# Anna's Home
# by the River

*This Book Proudly Owned*

*By* _____

**Third Edition 2009**

This "Gift of History" was made possible
with generous contributions from the following:

The Disneyland Resort
Brookfield Homes
Extron Electronics
Bill Taormina-Clean City, Inc.

# MY FAVORITE...

Animal _____

Book _____

Best friend _____

Color _____

Food _____

Place to visit _____

Song _____

Teacher _____

Thing to do _____

TV Show _____

What do you want to be when you grow up?

_____

_____

If you were Mayor for a day, what would you do?

_____

_____

# Anna's Home by the River

## A Children's History of Anaheim

by
**Gail Eastman**

Illustrated by
**Bob Bates**

Tesoro Publishing
Fullerton, California
2009

*Anna's Home by the River*

**Anna's Home by the River**
Tesoro Publishing
Post Office Box 528
Fullerton, California 92836
www.tesoropublishing.com

ISBN 978-0-9797419-0-6

First Edition, October 2007
Second Edition, September 2008
Third Edition, August 2009

Every effort has been made to produce a dependable history book based on information gathered from news articles, reference books and interviews. Although every attempt was made to be as accurate as possible, Tesoro Publishing does not make any representation that this book is free from error.

Tesoro Publishing supports educational programs and students by contributing to scholarships and local schools.

Anna's Home by the River
Authored by Gail Eastman
Illustrated by Bob Bates
Book Design by Helen Butler Graphics

Library of Congress Catalog Card Number: application pending

Printed in the United States of America

# Dedication

To the children of Anaheim
Who will determine the city's future

In loving memory of Elizabeth "Betty" Townsend
Mom – Teacher

To my grandchildren
Amanda, Alexandra, Brent, Drew and Sarah
A new generation
To study, then love and preserve history

# Acknowledgements

I would like to thank the following individuals for their indispensable contributions to the completion of this project: Chris Lowe and Emily Roberts of Tesoro Publishing for giving me the opportunity to write about Anaheim's history and for believing in my ability to do it. From the girls at the gym who encouraged me to start the project to my friends at CBS who kept me in their prayers the whole time, you're all part of this. Special thanks to Marcia who lent me her ear and always encouraged me. A big thanks to local historian Stephen Faessel and history room curator Jane Newell for their generosity in reviewing to make sure the historic content is correct. Jane, Opal Kissinger, Ymelda Ventura and Sal Addotta from the history room all worked to make sure pictures were located and scanned. The hours of review and critique by Anaheim third grade teacher Jennie Frank are beyond measure. For the feedback on selected chapters and the title given by special students and their parents, I'm grateful.

Thanks to the many authors who preserved Anaheim history in earlier books; they provided both facts and inspiration for this book.

The list of reference materials used includes many works by the late Dr. Leo J. Friis, *History of the Schmidt Family* by Richard D. Curtiss, *Dreams to Reality: A Profile of Modern Day Anaheim* by authors Black and Colson, and finally *Biographical Sketches of Anaheim* by the Anaheim Historical Society. To all the Anaheim Historical Society members for their love of history and everything they do to support it. Some of you are quoted, while others, like the Criss sisters, Virginia and Margie, continue to encourage and inspire younger Anaheim citizens to love the history of their city.

A special thanks to Anaheim Mayor Curt Pringle for his contribution to the project. Vicki Green, your editorial expertise and creative support as editor proved invaluable to me. Thank you to Bob Bates for your creative illustrations, the Anaheim History Room for photos which brought the text to life, and to Helen Butler for her graphic design talent in putting all our work together for readers to enjoy.

Last, but not least, to my husband Ron for his patience, and support, during the hours spent in research, writing and then what seemed like endless editing.

# Foreword

Few cities in the world have as much to offer as our city of Anaheim. We are lucky to live in a city that is blessed with great weather, a strong economy and a world-wide destination point that brings millions of visitors to our town each year.

Although Anaheim began as an agricultural community, the city's population began to boom after World War II. Growth continued after a visionary man named Walt Disney carved out 160 acres of orange groves and walnut trees in the early 1950s and began to build his vision for a family entertainment park. In fact, in 2007, Anaheim celebrated its sesquicentennial—the 150th anniversary of the city we call "home."

While people travel from around the world to visit our city, we know that Anaheim has much more to offer than just family entertainment. We have a strong and diverse economy. We have wonderful neighborhoods where children attend good schools, play in the parks and check out books from their local library. We also enjoy the presence of several major sports teams, which unite Anaheim residents as we enjoy these sporting events together.

Children who grow up in Anaheim have tremendous opportunity. I can not think of a better place to be a kid than Anaheim. I have lived in the Garden Grove/Anaheim area for more than 30 years. My wife and my two children were born in Anaheim. I am proud to have raised my own family here.

Our city has much to offer children growing up in Anaheim. Whether you dream of being a teacher, a businessperson, an astronaut, a doctor or the mayor, Anaheim can help you achieve that dream. Whether you visit the library, learn from your teachers, visit an art museum, play with your friends, attend a city council meeting, attend an Angels baseball or Ducks hockey game, Anaheim's culture and sense of community can help you learn about the world and yourself.

You can discover more about Anaheim's history—and the people who helped make our city great—in this book. Perhaps one day, grade school children will be reading about your dreams and achievements in a book just like this!

Curt Pringle
Mayor, City of Anaheim

# Anna's Home by the River
The History of Anaheim
Chapter book for 3rd grade Social Studies

# Table of Contents

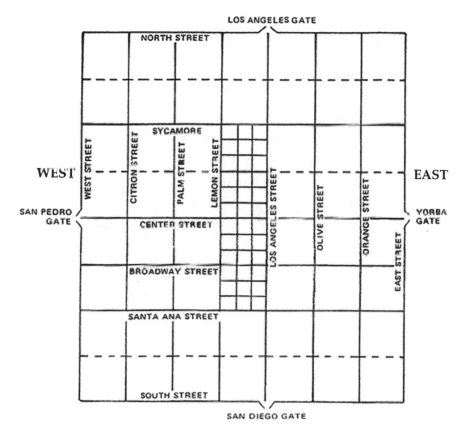

NORTH

LOS ANGELES GATE

NORTH STREET

SYCAMORE

WEST     EAST

SAN PEDRO GATE    YORBA GATE

CENTER STREET

BROADWAY STREET

SANTA ANA STREET

SOUTH STREET

SAN DIEGO GATE

SOUTH

*Map of the Mother Colony*

# CHAPTER 1
# Anaheim's First Residents
## (6000–8000 BC)

This story begins thousands of years ago. Wild animals lived on the land that is now Anaheim. The bones of mammoths, wolves, saber-tooth cats, and lions have all been found in Orange County.

Native Americans were the first human residents. No one knows for sure when they arrived. **Archaeologists** who studied their bones think they came to California between 6000 and 8000 BC.

Shoshoneans, Acjachemem or Tongva Indians all lived in this part of California. In their language, "Tongva" means "people of the Earth." Tongva people lived all over Los Angeles and Orange counties.

The Tongva Indians lived in small villages of 20 to 100 people. One of their villages was called "Hotuuknga." It was located by the Santa Ana River, where it runs through Anaheim.

Each family in the village had a house called a "kicha." Kicha's are dome-shaped houses built halfway underground. They were built with a frame of bent willow trees, covered by reeds. The floors were hard-packed dirt. In the center of the roof was a hole for light. It also let out smoke from their fire. When houses got old, they burned them and built new ones.

For food, the native people hunted wild animals and gathered plants, roots, and seeds. Acorns from oaks trees were important. A **mortar** and **pestle** were used to crush acorns and grind them into coarse meal.

Tannic acid in the acorn meal made it taste bad. They poured boiling water over the meal to filter out the bad taste. A **porridge** called "wewish" and a tortilla-like bread were made from the cooked meal.

The men were hunters. They hunted antelope and deer with bow and arrows. Smaller game like rabbits and birds were trapped. When the village was near water, they fished.

Native Americans did not wear many clothes in the summer. The women wore a two-piece apron. It was made from deerskin or a woven material made from plants called tule. Men wore just a belt to hang their tools and food on. Children didn't wear clothes until they were older. They went barefoot or wore sandals made from yucca leaves and string. In the winter, they wore capes made from rabbit fur, deerskin, or sea otter skin. They also slept on the fur skins.

Everyone had long, straight, black hair and tattoos. Tattoos were made by using cactus thorns to make cuts on their skin. The cuts were symbols or pictures. Then plant juice or charcoal was rubbed on the cuts to color the tattoos. Women wore necklaces and bracelets made from flowers, shells, and feathers.

Most Native Americans traveled on foot. Sometimes natives used large wood canoes in the ocean. Fish and **abalone** were caught in the ocean for food. They traveled as far as Santa Catalina Island to trade with natives there. A soft stone found on the Island was called soapstone. They used soapstone to make cooking pots and they used abalone shells for dishes.

Native American villages had their own government. The chief was in charge of keeping peace in his village. He was also the spiritual leader who preserved their holy symbols. When he died, his oldest son, or daughter, replaced him.

The second most important person in the village was the "shaman," or medicine man. His job was to cure sick people and bring luck to hunters. Storytellers and dancers were important because they preserved the culture and history for the next generation.

# CHAPTER 2

# Leather-jackets Find California
## (1542–1769)

In the 1500s, not long after Columbus discovered the New World, Spain conquered Mexico and Peru. That was the beginning of trading between Mexico, Asia, and Spain.

Everyone believed there was a water shortcut to China between the Pacific and Atlantic oceans. They named it the Strait of Anián. Explorers expected to find the shortcut north of Mexico, but never did. An explorer is a person who searches for new places.

The king of Spain sent the explorer Juan Rodriguez Cabrillo north from Mexico to find the shortcut. His first stop was a bay now called San Diego. He claimed it for Spain, which ruled it for the next 300 years.

Cabrillo continued north, where he discovered and claimed Monterey Bay. He never found a shortcut to Asia, but he is considered one of the founding fathers of California because of his discoveries.

Fifty years later, another explorer named Sebastián Vizcaíno reached Monterey Bay. Then Spain's King Carlos decided South America was a more valuable

Courtesy of the Irvine Company

*Early explorers*

place to explore. No one came back to explore California again for 167 years.

In 1769, Spain sent explorers to California again because they heard that the Russians were exploring the coast south of Alaska. The explorers were ordered to claim the land for Spain. They built missions and presidios to protect the land from other nations' claims. The forts where the soldiers lived were called presidios.

The most famous explorer to reach San Diego was Don Gaspar de Portolà. In July 1769, he started north with an expedition of about 70 men. They entered what is now Orange County, near the site of Mission San Juan Capistrano.

*Portolà*

The soldiers were called "leather-jackets" because they wore sleeveless shirts called **jerkins**. Jerkins were made from six layers of deerskin to protect against arrows. They carried a bull-hide shield and were armed with a steel spear called a **lance.** They also carried a broadsword and a musket.

Father Juan Crespi was a padre, or priest, who traveled with Portolà.

Courtesy of the First American Title Corporation

*Padres on trails traveling between missions*

Sergeant José Francisco Ortega was their scout. A man sent out ahead to find the best travel route was called a scout. The trip was hard with no maps or roads to follow. Each day, the scout traveled ahead to make a trail and find fresh water.

# CHAPTER 3

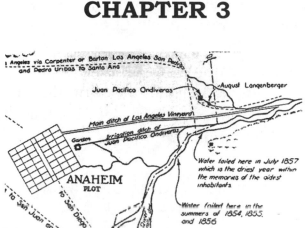

# The Earthquake River

People sometimes wonder where some of the unusual names in Orange County come from. Places were often named after people or events. It was the custom to name places as explorers traveled over new lands.

Don Gaspar de Portolá's expedition camped on a mcsa, or flat hilltop, north of San Juan Canyon. One of the soldiers lost his gun on the mesa. The gun was called a **Trabuco rifle**. They named that place Trabuco Mesa.

Later that name was also used for a canyon and a road near the mesa. Ortega Highway was named after the expedition's scout Sergeant Ortega.

Before leaving the mesa, they celebrated the Feast Day of Saint Anne. To honor the Saint, they named the valley Santa Ana and they named the hills the Santa Ana Mountains.

Courtesy of the First American Title Corporation

*Portolà's expedition had to cross many rivers*

A few days later, they arrived at the east bank of a large, fast moving river. The Earth shook with violent earthquakes before they crossed it. Father Crespi named the river "The River of the Sweet Name of Jesus of the Earthquakes." That was hard for everyone to remember. So, the soldiers just called it the Santa Ana River or "El Rio de Santa Ana" in Spanish.

Today, you can walk or ride a bike on a path along that river. The path goes from Anaheim's eastern border past Anaheim Stadium.

You may not see much water in the river during the summer. During the winter rains, it fills up with fast-moving water that flows from the Santa Ana Mountains.

# CHAPTER 4

# The California Missions
## (1769–1823)

When explorers came to California in 1769, padres traveled with them to build missions in San Diego and Monterey. They wanted to teach the Native Americans about Christianity.

The king of Spain wanted more missions built. They were all built a day's ride apart on horse back, so travelers could stop along their journey for food and supplies.

Many Native American Indians came to the missions for gifts of glass beads or colorful cloth from the Spaniards. The Spaniards did not bring many workers with them to help. They used the Native Americans to build the missions. Once they came to the missions to work, the Spaniards did not let them leave. They forced them to live and work there.

Two California missions are the most important to the history of Anaheim and to Orange County. The closest mission to Anaheim is called Mission San Gabriel Archangel, which is near Los Angeles. The second is Mission San Juan Capistrano, located near the southern border of the county.

*Mission San Gabriel*

The Spanish named the Native American Indians after the mission they lived near. The Tongva Native Americans who lived in the area that is now Anaheim were called Gabrieleños after the San Gabriel mission. The Tongva people who lived in the southern area were called Juaneños because they lived near the San Juan Capistrano Mission.

Courtesy of the Placentia History Room

*Mission San Juan Capistrano*

The padres at the San Gabriel Mission used the Gabrieleños to help build their mission. While the Gabrieleños lived inside the mission, the men were taught blacksmithing, brick making, and leather tanning. Those skills were useful for building and making wagons, tools, and shoes. Some of the men were taught to ride horses. They became cowboys, or **vaqueros**, who cared for the cattle.

Women learned how to make olive oil, wine, candles, and soap. They were also trained in sewing, weaving, and cooking. Everyone worked in the fields where wheat, corn, beans, and a variety of fruits were grown.

The padres taught the Native Americans to speak Spanish and tried to convert them to **Catholicism**. Some wanted to, but most did not. To help convince them to become Catholics, Spain promised the Native Americans that they could own land.

Courtesy of The First American Title Corporation

*Padres converted many Native Americans to Catholicism*

Many of the Spanish explorers and soldiers married Native American women. They settled nearby to farm and raise cattle. The farms destroyed the Native Americans traditional food-gathering grounds.

That caused more Native Americans to move into the missions for food.

*Courtesy of the Placentia History Room*

*Typical room in an early California mission*

Living conditions were crowded at the mission. The Gabrieleños living there were exposed to new diseases brought by the Spanish. Many became sick and died from diseases like measles and chicken pox. Others died from being forced to work too hard.

About half the Native Americans died in the first 65 years of mission life. There are now only a few Gabrieleño Native American descendents left in all of Orange County.

# CHAPTER 5

Courtesy of the California History Room, California State University, Sacramento, California

# The Rancho Period
## (1800–1864)

All the land in Anaheim was once part of three **ranchos**, or ranches, owned by only three families.

When land in California was ruled by Spain, the king gave **concessions**, or a **grant** of land, to a few soldiers as rewards for their service. That meant they had permission to use the land as long as they built a house and lived there. They were also required to raise cattle.

Courtesy of the Anaheim History Room

*Nieto Grant*

The first Spanish concession of land in Orange County was all the land from the San Gabriel River to the Santa Ana River. It was called the Nieto Grant because it was given to a Spaniard named Manuel Nieto in 1794.

When Mexico took over rule, the rancho families were given land grants. The grants from Mexico gave them ownership rights. That allowed them to sell parts of their land.

A Spaniard, Juan Pablo Grijalva, was given a land grant in 1802. That land is now a big part of Orange County. He named his rancho "El Rancho Santiago de Santa Ana." He built a **hacienda**, or house, and lived there with his family. His daughter married a soldier from Portolà's expedition, Jose Antonio Yorba.

When Grijalva died, Yorba and his nephew took over the rancho. The nephew was Juan Pablo Peralta. Together, they managed this large rancho with many cowboys. Their land included cities we know today as Orange, Santa Ana, Tustin, Costa Mesa, and Newport Beach. Part of east Anaheim and Anaheim Hills are also on land included in the Yorba rancho.

Don Bernardo Yorba was Jose Antonio Yorba's third son. He received a land grant from the governor of Mexico in 1834 for "Rancho Canon de Santa Ana." His rancho was north of the Santa Ana River.

Courtesy of the Placentia History Room

*Don Bernardo Yorba*

Don Bernardo's rancho included part of today's Anaheim and all of Yorba Linda. He was very rich and had a large family of 20 children! With so many children, his rancho even had a one-room school.

The third rancho was owned by Juan Pacifico Ontiveros. Ontiveros was the grandson of one of the first soldiers. He received a Mexican land grant for the rancho he named "Rancho San Juan Cajon de Santa Ana." It was northwest of the Santa Ana River. Today,

Courtesy of the Placentia History Room

*Juan Pacifico Ontiveros and his wife Martina Ontiveros*

35

the cities of Fullerton, Brea, Placentia, and part of Anaheim are on that land.

In 1855, a **civil engineer** from Los Angeles named George Hansen **surveyed** the Ontiveros land to confirm their grant from the

Mexican government. During that time he met the owners, Juan Pacifico Ontiveros, his wife Martina, and their German-born son-in-law, August Langenberger. They all lived on the rancho. George Hansen returned in 1857 to purchase land from the Ontiveros rancho that was to become Anaheim.

Courtesy of the Anaheim History Room
*August Langenberger*

# CHAPTER 6

Courtesy of the Placentia History Room

# Roundups and Reatas
## (1800–1864)

Ranchos were much like small villages. The owner's and the worker's families all lived on the rancho. Many of the workers and cowboys were Gabrieleños who had left the mission. The main business of the rancho was raising cattle.

Some farming was done on the grounds surrounding the houses. Wheat and corn were grown in large fields. Close to the rancho buildings, they planted vegetable gardens, fruit trees, and grapevines. They raised food for everyone living on the rancho.

Ranchos had no fences. Cattle roamed everywhere. Each rancho had its own **brand** to mark their cattle. The brand told everyone who owned the cattle.

Every spring, the ranchos held a roundup. Cowboys used their skill with horses and used **reatas** as lassos to round up the cattle. The reata was a braided leather rope. A 50-foot long reata was also used to measure land. Two vaqueros on horseback stretched it between two poles to measure the boundaries of a rancho's land. The measurements were used to draw a diseno, or map, of the rancho.

During the roundup the cattle were separated by each ranchos' brand. Then calves were branded by their owners. They picked out the cattle to use on the rancho. The rest of the herd was set free to roam for another year.

Extra cattle were **slaughtered** for trading. Meat, hides, and tallow from the cattle were traded for things like gold, silver, fine furniture, beautiful cloth, and spices. Tallow is a hard white fat that was used to make soap and candles.

When the roundup was finished, they celebrated with a "fiesta," or big party. After the fiesta, each family and their vaqueros drove their cattle back to their rancho.

They also held fiestas on special occasions or feast days. Some guests came from far away on horseback or by ox cart. Fiestas usually began with church services. Everyone was dressed in their finest clothes. After church, they started with a feast. Then sports, games, music, and dancing would begin. Sometimes the fiestas lasted for many days.

Courtesy of the Santa Ana History Room

*Typical fiesta clothing*

The Spanish thought it was important to be good citizens and good Christians. Children were taught by their parents and the padres to be truthful and kind. They were also taught to be polite and always keep their promises. Girls were taught by their mothers how to care for the household. Boys were taught by their fathers to ride horses and run the rancho.

Most rancho families were not as wealthy or as large as the Yorba family. They did not have schoolhouses on their ranchos. Older children were sometimes sent away to live at **boarding schools**. When schools were built in towns, the rancho children attended them. Four Spanish-speaking children from the ranchos attended Anaheim's first school in the fall of 1860.

Many rancho owners sold part of their land for settlements. That left less room for the cattle to roam the hillsides. The end of the ranchos came in 1864 after two years of drought. When it does not rain for a very long time people call it a **drought**. That drought caused most of the rancho cattle to die of thirst or starvation.

# CHAPTER 7

# The Golden State
## (1845–1850)

In the mid-1800s, the United States defeated Mexico in a war fought over the territory of Texas. When the war ended, Mexico gave the northern half of their land to the United States. That land became a new United States territory. Land that is now the state of California was included in the new territory. A **treaty**, or agreement, allowed Mexican citizens to keep the land grants they had been given.

Once California was part of the United States, many settlers came from the east. On January 24, 1848, a carpenter named James Wilson Marshall was inspecting a **mill** owned by Johann August Sutter. He saw something glittering behind a stone in the water. Marshall's discovery turned out to be gold.

News of the gold discovery quickly spread around the world. Californians rushed to where the gold was found. Stories were told of gold nuggets as big as hen's eggs found in the American River near Sutter's Mill.

Thousands of people came from all over the world to search for gold. They came by ship around South America or by covered wagon on trails across the continent. At that time, San Francisco was the largest city in California. Many people arrived there by ship on their way to the gold fields.

Miners who came to California in the gold rush of 1849 were called forty-niners. They worked day and night sifting through mud in the rivers to find gold. It was hard work. Conditions were very hard. Many quickly packed up and returned to their former jobs in the city. Many stayed in San Francisco or moved to Los Angeles.

In 1848, a group of 48 Californians met as **delegates** to a Constitutional Convention. They gathered to write a **constitution** for California so that it could become a state. Eight of them were Spanish-speaking rancho owners. All 48 men had lived in California for more than three years. Almost half of them were younger than 35 years old. Many important decisions were made by those men.

First, they asked the United States Congress to allow California to become a state. Most states were territories before they became a state. They also decided to make California a "free" state. That meant that no one could own other people as slaves.

A third big decision was to allow married women to own property. Under Mexican rule, women could own property. That decision made California the first state in the United States to allow women to be property owners.

On September 9, 1850, California became the 31st state. After four years, the delegates finally chose Sacramento as the state capitol.

# CHAPTER 8

# What Happened
# to the Willow Fence?
## (1857–1859)

John Frohling and Charles Kohler were friends and partners in a Los Angeles **vineyard** and winery. They dreamed of expanding their business.

From that dream came the idea to organize a farm community to grow grapes and make wine. They shared their idea with George Hansen who decided to join them. He was an experienced surveyor who knew the land around Los Angeles. A surveyor looks at the land, then measures it and marks it out for a map.

*Vineyard of Frohling & Kohler*

*Anaheim founder
George Hansen*

On February 24, 1857, they shared their dream with friends at a meeting in San Francisco. Many German immigrants who attended the meeting decided to join them. The group voted to form the Los Angeles Vineyard Society. Each person who joined **invested** money in the society. That investment was called a share. Fifty shares were sold. The money was used to buy land for the new **settlement**.

They elected Mr. Hansen as the **superintendent** of the Society. He was to purchase land, survey it, and then divide it into smaller sections. Then he supervised planting the grapes. Share owners planned to move to the settlement, tend the grapes, and make wine.

On September 12, 1857, Hansen and Frohling purchased 1,165 acres from Juan Pacifico Ontiveros and his wife Martina for two dollars an acre. Don

Bernard Yorba was paid $200 for the right t
a ditch over his land to supply water from
Santa Ana River.

Hansen divided the land
into farm lots of 20 acres
each. In the center were
half-acre town lots. Some
lots were reserved for
houses. The other lots were
for schools or public
buildings. Each lot was
given a letter and number.
Society members drew
numbers from a hat for the

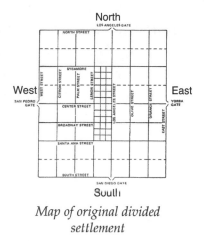

*Map of original divided
settlement*

land they would own. Each share owner got a 20-acre
farm section, plus a town lot. Some had invested more
money so they owned more than one share.

That same year, Hansen built Anaheim's first house
with redwood shipped from northern California. The
house was located at 235 North Los Angeles Street,

*Mother Colony House*

where he lived for
three years. Many
years later it was
moved to 414 North
West Street and is
known as the Mother
Colony House.
George Hansen is

47

known as the "Father of Anaheim" for the role he played in the founding of the city.

Before vines were planted, a fence had to be built around the town to keep out roaming cattle and wild animals. Hansen hired Native Americans, Mexicans, and a few Germans to build the fence and plant vines. They gathered 40,000 willow branches from the river for the fence.

Roads around the settlement were named North, South, East, and West. Each road had a gate into the colony named for the city or ranch in that direction. To the north was the Los Angeles Gate, or North Gate. The San Diego Gate was on the south. The Yorba Gate was on the east, and the San Pedro Gate was on the west. They could be closed and locked at night to keep out animals.

In a short time those willow branches rooted and grew into trees! The trees used too much water, which was needed for the grapes. The trees were cut down and used for firewood. Cactus replaced the fence and cowboys patrolled the roads to keep the cattle out.

# CHAPTER 9

Courtesy of the Anaheim History Room

# Anna's Home by the River
## 1858

Over the years there have been different stories
about how the city got its name. Before settlers
arrived, Spanish-speaking neighbors called the
settlement "Campo Alemán," or German Camp.

On January 15, 1858, the Society members
gathered in San Francisco to choose a name for their
new settlement. Many names were suggested, so they
voted to choose one. The vote was between
Annaheim, Annagau, and Weinheim. On the first
ballot there was no majority. When a second ballot
was taken, Annaheim won by two votes.

You may notice it was spelled with two "n's" in the beginning. No one knows for sure why, but after a few months, one was dropped, and the spelling officially became Anaheim.

The word "heim" means home in German. The "Ana" part came from the name of the Santa Ana River. So the name Anaheim was said to mean "home by the river." The name was suggested by pioneer Theodore E. Schmidt.

Courtesy of the Anaheim History Room
*Theodore E. Schmidt*

In 1860, the first child was born in the new settlement. She was named Anna in honor of their new hometown. Her father, John Fischer, was the first secretary of the Vineyard Society in San Francisco. He also served as Anaheim's first postmaster and the third mayor.

When Anna was eight-years-old, her father opened the Planters Hotel. It may have been around that time when

Courtesy of the Anaheim History Room
*Anna Fischer (left) and Nellie Kuchel (right)*

**mischievous** little Anna Fischer began telling visitors that Anaheim was named after her.

Like any **fib** that is often repeated, people sometimes begin believing it is true. People started believing that the city really was named after Anna Fisher. In fact, years later an official United States government publication told Anna's version of how the city got its name. In 1905, a Gazette story pointed out that the story could not be true since the name Anaheim was chosen in 1858, which was two years before little Anna was even born!

In spite of the real facts, some people still believed the city was named after the little girl named Anna. Now you know the true story of how Anaheim got its name and what the name means.

Courtesy of the Anaheim History Room

*The Planters Hotel*

# CHAPTER 10

Courtesy of the Anaheim History Room

# A Steamship Delivers
## (1859–1870)

It was two years after land was purchased before settlers began arriving from San Francisco. The vineyards were planted with 400,000 healthy, fast-growing Mission grapes.

A steamship named the Senator brought the settlers as far as the San Pedro Harbor. Because the harbor was shallow, the Senator anchored three miles out in the ocean.

Small boats, also called lighters, were used to transfer the settlers and supplies in shallow water. The boats were rowed through waves toward the beach. Finally, strong Native Americans carried people and cargo to shore on their shoulders. Once on land, it was 25 miles to Anaheim. The trail was rough, and it took a long time in horse-drawn wagons.

The first building they saw in 1859 was still under construction. It was the two-story Langenberger & Co. adobe general store. August Langenberger and his partner, Benjamin Dreyfus, opened their first store that year, right in the center of town.

Courtesy of the Anaheim History Room

*Langenberger & Co. adobe general store*

Since the town had hardly any houses, the new settlers lived in tents. Construction of houses started right away with redwood lumber they brought with them.

Most colonists had been businessmen or artists. John Frohling was the only one experienced in both farming and winemaking.

Anaheim's vineyards were soon known as the finest in Los Angeles County. Only four years after planting, they were producing excellent wines. By the mid-1860s, the wines were even well known outside of California. They won awards for their quality.

Courtesy of the Anaheim History Room
*Zanjero and his horse*

The Anaheim Water Company was formed in 1859 to supply water to the vineyards. A "zanjero," or water steward, was hired to make sure the ditch, or "zanja," was in good condition so water could reach the vineyards.

Anaheim's first doctor came to town in 1862, traveling by wagon train from Mexico. His name was John Heyermann. The wagon train was attacked by Apache Indians along the way. When they reached Anaheim, the doctor was so happy to meet fellow Germans that he decided to stay and open a drugstore.

That same year, all but one resident survived the settlement's first great flood. After 30 days of rain, water covered most of the town. It was higher than the children's waists in some places. Vineyards were damaged, and many **adobe** buildings were washed away.

After the flood of 1862, there was a drought that lasted two years. The settlers had to hire vaqueros to keep thirsty cattle out of their vineyards. Even during the drought, grapes thrived and wine production increased.

Courtesy of the Anaheim History Room

*Thriving vineyard*

# CHAPTER 11

Courtesy of the Anaheim History Room

## Anaheim's Schools
### (1859–2009)

During the settlers' first year in the colony, a public school was started. Frederick W. Kuelp was a teacher who owned a share in the Vineyard Society, but he still lived in San Francisco. The settlers talked him into moving his family to Anaheim in early 1860 to become the first teacher.

Courtesy of the Anaheim History Room
*Frederick W. Kuelp*

Classes were held in a small Indian adobe lodge behind the Langenberger store. Nine students were in the first class. Five of them spoke only German. Four students came from the ranchos outside town and spoke only Spanish. It was the law that classes be taught in English. That helped everyone learn English together.

Settlers built a small adobe school at 124 Elm Street. It was also a home for the teacher and his family. In 1862, the first big flood washed away the school. The Kuelps lost their home and their furniture, including a valuable piano.

After the flood, school classes were held in a small room on the second floor of the Langenberger store. Later, classes moved back to the old Indian adobe near the store. By 1870, there were 91 students.

With so many students, Anaheim still needed a new school building, but there was no money for one. The school's third teacher was a Civil War veteran

*Central School*

*James M. Guinn*

named James M. Guinn. He had the idea for the city to sell school bonds to raise money for building schools. Buying a bond is a way for someone to invest their money. His school bond idea was made into a State law in 1878 and he became famous for that. Central School in Anaheim was the first California school built with money from the new school bond law.

*Children attend Central School, 1899*

As the population grew, many new schools were built. In the early years, schools were often named for their location, like Central School. Sometimes they were named for the street they were on, like Loara or Sunkist schools.

Courtesy of the Anaheim History Room

*Thomas Jefferson School, 1940; Loara School, 1960; Benjamin Franklin School, 1970 (top to bottom)*

It was also customary in the early 1900s for schools to be named after famous people from history. Abraham Lincoln, Benjamin Franklin, Thomas Edison, and Patrick Henry are some historic names used for Anaheim schools.

Guinn Elementary School was named to honor the pioneer teacher, James M. Guinn. In later years, other schools were named to honor special people in local history. A former school nurse, Adelaide Price, and a superintendent, Melbourne Gauer, each have schools named after them.

Courtesy of the Anaheim History Room

*Adelaide Price and Melbourne Gauer*

Do you know how your school got its name?

# CHAPTER 12

Courtesy of the Anaheim History Room

# From Bricks to Buildings
## (1865–1880)

The small settlement of Anaheim was becoming a real town. By 1865, there was a post office, a Wells Fargo stagecoach office, and two general stores. They supplied everything the small town needed.

The first industry to build and hire many workers was a brickyard. Many of Anaheim's first buildings were built of brick. Dozens of carpenters, painters, and four bricklayers were kept busy.

The list of tradesmen included saddle makers, shoemakers, tailors, and a barber. Shops were opened by a blacksmith, a wagon maker, and a tinsmith who made buckets. "Professor" J.H.T. Dean was an African American who owned one of the town's early barber shops. People could get a haircut, a shave, and a hot bath at his Anaheim Shaving Salon in 1872.

Places for social gatherings were also important. A restaurant, two **saloons**, and a billiard saloon—or pool hall—were the most popular places. Many of the original colonists were musicians. They formed a band and a singing society with 22 members.

Courtesy of the Anaheim History Room

*Anaheim City Band*

St. Michael's Episcopal Church held its first meetings on the second floor of a saloon downtown.

In 1866, the Anaheim Cemetery was opened east of town. It is the oldest public cemetery in Orange County. Many of the original settlers and their descendents are buried there. Before that time, people were buried in small family plots on their own land.

*The old Anaheim Cemetery entrance on Center Street*

Merchants needed a closer place than San Pedro for the shipment of goods. The answer was a spot only 17 miles away. It was Alamitos Bay, near the mouth of the San Gabriel River. A group of settlers built a pier there to unload goods. They called it Anaheim Landing.

*Anaheim Landing, a popular seaside resort*

The Anaheim Lighter Company was formed to transfer goods by small boats from shore to ships. The boat company was successful until the railroads arrived in Anaheim. Then, Anaheim Landing became a popular seaside resort.

By the late 1860s, two first-class hotels were built in Anaheim. The Anaheim Hotel and The Planters Hotel opened with such luxuries as hot and cold running water. They even had an ice-making machine so they could serve ice cream.

Courtesy of the Anaheim History Room

*Anaheim Hotel, 1871-1872*

Anaheim incorporated as the "Town of Anaheim" on February 10, 1870. A City Hall was built with offices for the Police Department, which included two jail cells. Just two years later, the city was unincorporated because it ran out of money. Anaheim reincorporated December 6, 1876. In 1888, the town was reorganized again as a **general law city**. A general

law city is allowed by the state to make some of their own laws.

Major Max Strobel was elected in 1870 as the first mayor. He wanted Los Angeles County to be split in half, with the land south of the San Gabriel River to become the County of Anaheim. The **state legislature** did not like that idea

Courtesy of the Anaheim History Room

*Major Max Strobel, first mayor of Anaheim*

and said no. Finally, in 1889, Los Angeles County did split in half, but the new county south of the river was called Orange County rather than Anaheim.

At first the town's water supply came from the river through ditches. Homeowners added wells and **windmills** to pump drinking water.

Courtesy of the Anaheim History Room

*Dietrich Strodthoff home with a windmill on N. Lemon Street*

On September 15, 1879 the Anaheim Water Department started the first water-pumping plant on Cypress Street. It was between Los Angeles Street (today's Anaheim Boulevard) and Lemon Street. Anaheim still owns the system that supplies water to its residents.

Courtesy of the Anaheim History Room

*. Water pumping plant*

# CHAPTER 13

Courtesy of the Anaheim History Room

# People, Trains, and Street Racing
## (1870–1880)

The vineyards and wineries became so successful that more help was needed in the fields. In 1870, the first Chinese laborers came to Anaheim from San Francisco. They worked on the water ditches first and then in the vineyards. Those workers founded Orange County's first Chinatown, just north of downtown Anaheim along Chartres Street. Chinatown was there for more than 50 years.

Courtesy of the Anaheim History Room

*Handyman Ah Foo*

During the early 1900s, everyone in town knew Ah Foo, the Chinese handyman.

The Anaheim Gazette was the first newspaper published in the area outside Los Angeles. Early in the 1870s, Henry Kuchel delivered those first papers when he was 11-years-old. When he grew up, he bought the paper and became its **editor**. He was the first person from Southern California to be in the California Newspaper Hall of Fame.

The first rail line to reach Anaheim was the Southern Pacific Railroad in 1875. The first tourist came to town before the passenger depot was even finished. A sight-seeing train arrived at the spot on the west side of town where they were building the

Courtesy of the Anaheim History Room

*Henry Kuchel*

72

depot. A monument now marks that spot at Broadway and Manchester Avenue.

Courtesy of the Anaheim History Room

*1875 Southern Pacific depot; renamed the West Anaheim train station in 1907*

The number of trains arriving in town grew fast. Stages and horses racing up Center Street from the train depot became a problem. A newspaper story said "street racing" endangered ladies and children. It described the racing drivers as "some **ignoramus** who only has sense enough to hang on to a pair of lines." Ignoramus is an old fashioned word used to describe a person who is ignorant or not educated.

A few years later, the location of the Southern Pacific depot was changed. A new depot was built at the corner of Santa Ana Street and Los Angeles Street.

Courtesy of the Anaheim History Room

*1899 Southern Pacific depot on Santa Ana Street at Los Angeles Street*

The station is gone, but **freight trains** still travel those tracks in the middle of Santa Ana Street.

Courtesy of the Anaheim History Room

*Friedrich Conrad*

Anaheim's first beer was made at the California Brewery owned by pioneer Friedrich Conrad. The city's first amusement park was also started by Conrad in 1876. It was called Tivoli Gardens, named after a famous park in Denmark.

Tivoli Gardens didn't have rides like Disneyland. It had things like a bowling alley, a shooting gallery, and lawns for croquet. The most popular part was a dance pavilion and beer garden

Courtesy of the Anaheim History Room

*Anaheim Brewery*

where people could drink Anaheim beer and dance to live music.

Anaheim's first celebrity, Madame Helena Modjeska, arrived in 1876. She was an actress. Her husband, Polish Count Karol Bozenta Chlapowski, and their son Rudolphe, were with her. They came with a group from Poland to establish an **immigrant** farm community.

Courtesy of the Anaheim History Room

*Madame Helena Modjeska, actress*

They soon found out they did not make good farmers. Madame Modjeska returned to acting and traveled the United States performing. She continued to visit her friends who were from many of Anaheim's pioneer families.

Madame Modjeska built a home in a Santa Ana mountain canyon for her retirement. She called it Arden. That canyon became known as Modjeska Canyon in her honor. The house and gardens are now an Orange County historic site open to visitors.

*Early St. Boniface, church (left); Presbyterians built the first Protestant church in Orange County (below)*

Courtesy of the Anaheim History Room

St. Boniface was the first church in town. Their first building was built in 1870 on Cypress Street.

In 1873 the Presbyterians built the first Protestant church in Orange County. It was on the corner of Los Angeles Street and Cypress Street. Later the building was moved to the corner of Cypress and Claudina Streets where it was enlarged. It is still used as a church today.

# CHAPTER 14

Courtesy of the Anaheim History Room

# Grapes, Oranges, and Chili Peppers
## (1880–1900)

Suddenly, in the early 1880s, the grapevines began to die. People thought it was because of bad weather or bad soil. Experts were called. No one could figure out the cause or a cure. They called it "The Anaheim Disease."

Finally, one expert, Newton B. Pierce, said it was a **bacterium**, or sickness, spread by leafhoppers. Leafhoppers are a family of small insects that eat plants and crops. Soon, all the grapes were dead. In the 1970s, modern scientific tests found out that Newton Pierce was right. Since then, it has been called "Pierce's Disease."

Farmers looking for crops to replace the grapes tried many other things. Walnuts and citrus trees grew well in Anaheim. Sugar beets and other vegetables did

*Workers in orange grove (above); drying walnuts at the Frank Edison ranch on N. East Street (right)*

Courtesy of the Anaheim History Room

too. A popular chili pepper was developed in Anaheim about that time. "Anaheim Chilies" are still grown locally and are a favorite with cooks.

Oranges proved to be the most profitable crop. Most of the farms and ranches around town started replacing other crops with orange trees. Packing houses were built near the railroad lines and Anaheim became known as the center for orange growing in the county.

"Ostrich farming" came to an area west of town with the arrival of strange-looking "camel-birds" from South Africa. They were raised for their beautiful feathers, which were used on women's hats and clothing. The feathers from just one bird were worth $400.

Courtesy of the Anaheim History Room

*Ostrich farm*

An Anaheim barber and the postman were the first men known to harness and race ostriches.

They hitched them behind a special kind of cart, called a sulky, for racing against a horse. Their birds were named Napoleon and Bonaparte.

They joined a traveling circus with those birds. Ostriches can be very hard to control and sometimes very mean birds. One day, the postman was kicked

Courtesy of the Anaheim History Room

*Billy Frantz the barber (left) and Frank Eastman the postman (right)*

in the head by one of the birds. It almost knocked him silly.

*Frank Eastman and his mail cart, 1898*

Courtesy of the Anaheim History Room

After that, both the postman and barber wanted to go back to a safer and quieter life. They quit racing, left the circus, and returned to Anaheim without the funny-looking birds.

# CHAPTER 15

Courtesy of the Anaheim History Room

# Trolleys and Telephones
## (1888–1900)

Rumors that the Santa Fe Railroad line would come to town sparked a land boom in the 1880s. That prompted the founding of the Anaheim Streetcar Company to provide horse-drawn trolley service down Center Street. Once the Santa Fe train depot was built on the east side of town in 1888, the trolley ran between that depot and the Southern

Pacific Depot on the west side of town. The trolleys looked very much like the trolleys that carry visitors down Main Street in Disneyland.

When voters approved splitting Los Angeles County in half, Anaheim wanted to be picked for the new **county seat**. The county seat is the center for the county government and is where the courthouse is built. Instead of choosing Anaheim, their rival, Santa Ana, was picked.

Courtesy of the Anaheim History Room

*"The Gypsy" benefit performance of 1909 at Reiser' Opera House*

The town was growing up. Reiser's Opera House opened for live performances in a new brick theater. Cement sidewalks and a large two-story city hall were added on Center Street. About the same time, bicycles became the most popular transportation around town. Most people called bicycles a "wheel." Businessmen gave up their horses and rode their "wheels" around town or to work. Some girls even learned to ride them.

The voters approved building a city-owned power generating plant in 1895. That gave Anaheim electricity only 16 years after Thomas Edison invented the light bulb. Anaheim was one of the first cities in Southern California to supply electricity to its citizens.

Courtesy of the Anaheim History Room

*Interior of Anaheim's first electric power generating plant, 1895*

Only 35 people in Anaheim had telephones before 1900. Those telephones did not have dials, so an operator at a switchboard connected the calls.

Courtesy of the Anaheim History Room

*Maude Mickle Backs demonstrating Anaheim's first telephone switchboard*

The Sunset Telephone and Telegraph Company's switchboard was in a building on Center Street. Eight to 12 people shared what was called a "party line." Everyone on the party line could listen in on their neighbor's conversations. Even the operator listened in sometimes.

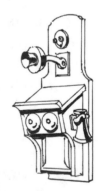

# CHAPTER 16

# Cars and the Candy Library
## (1900–1910)

Shortly after 1900, automobiles began to change what people in Anaheim did for fun. Families started enjoying Sunday drives in the country. The Anaheim Gazette reported that one owner of a new Ford car was seen driving east with a dog sitting on each running board and a cow in the back seat, with its head sticking out.

The Portolà expedition's original dirt trail between the missions was known as "El Camino Real," or "The King's Highway." It stretched from San Diego to Monterey. In Orange County, it passed through Tustin, Orange, and right down Los Angeles Street in Anaheim, and north through Fullerton.

Chris Lowe

*El Camino Real bell*

Beginning in 1906, the Automobile Club of Southern California put 450 mission bells by the side of the road to mark the El Camino Real. There were four bells on Los Angeles Street along Anaheim's part of the highway. They serve as reminders of the El Camino Real.

Anaheim's first public library was in Mr. Bruce's candy store on Center Street. People could borrow books and have sweets at the same place. Doesn't that sound like fun?

A famous businessman in the early 1900s believed every town should have a free library. That was Andrew

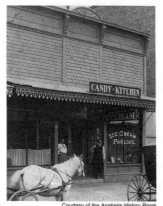

Courtesy of the Anaheim History Room

*Mr. Bruce's candy store*

88

Carnegie. He offered to give small towns all over America money to build libraries.

By that time, Anaheim's library had outgrown the candy store. City leaders asked Mr. Carnegie for help building a new library. In 1908, Mr. Carnegie gave Anaheim a grant for $10,000 to help build the library. A grant is like a gift except with conditions. The conditions with this grant

Courtesy of the Anaheim History Room

*Carnegie Library*

required the city to provide land for the building and money to operate the library.

Anaheim's Carnegie Library was built at the corner of Broadway and Los Angeles Street. Many people who grew up in Anaheim have special memories of visiting the children's room downstairs when they were young. It had a door next to the main entrance just for kids to go downstairs into their special room.

A larger, modern library was built a few blocks away in the 1960s to replace the Carnegie Library.

After the new library opened in December 1963, the old building was used for city offices. At one time

*Modern Anaheim Library*

it was even scheduled to be torn down. People who loved the old building joined together to preserve it. They helped turn it into a home for the Anaheim Museum. Now the building is even more special because it is the only Carnegie Library building in Orange County.

Today, people visit the old Carnegie Library and Anaheim's first house, the Mother Colony House, to learn more about history.

# Chapter 17

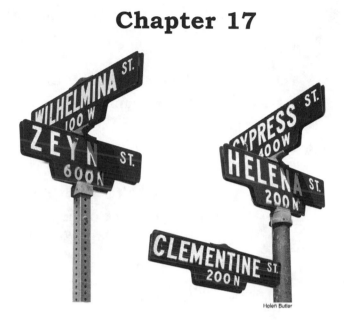

Holen Butler

# How the Streets
# Got Their Names

Many of Anaheim's first streets were named after
early pioneers. Some are named after pioneers' wives
or daughters. Adele, Claudina, and Wilhelmina were
popular names in the 1800s when they were used as
names for Anaheim streets.

Helena Street was named in honor of Madame
Helena Modjeska, the famous actress. Next to it is
Clementine Street, named after Helena's good friend,
Clementina Zimmerman Schmidt Langenberger.

*Clementina Zimmerman*

*John Zeyn*

*Henry Kroeger*

Ms. Langenberger was Anaheim's oldest and last pioneer. She died in 1913.

Others street names came from the last name of the men who first owned the land. Henry Kroeger and John Zeyn were both pioneer land owners. The streets named after them are on the land they once owned. Street names like Dickel and Stueckle honor prominent early families in the city.

Some streets are named for trees and flowers. Many people came to Anaheim from other states like Ohio, Indiana, and Illinois. Streets by those names in Anaheim are in the same order from east to west as the states appear on the map.

One wealthy rancher, Mr. John B. Rea, had two daughters. One daughter was named Kate and the other one was named Ella.

He combined their names to call his ranch "Katella." The road that passed by his ranch became

Courtesy of the Anaheim History Room

*Kate and Ella Rea*

Katella Avenue. An elementary school on that road was named Katella School. One of his daughters was a teacher in Anaheim schools for many years. When a new high school was built in the 1960s, it was named Katella High School.

Courtesy of the Anaheim History Room

*Katella High School, 1966*

Between 1914 and 1918 Germany was at war with many nations, including the United States. It was called World War I. At the time people thought the street names, like Hedwig, sounded too German. They were afraid someone would think German immigrants living in Anaheim were not loyal Americans. So the city changed the street name to a more **patriotic**-sounding name. That is how Hedwig Street became Philadelphia Street.

The tradition of name changing didn't stop there. Years later, Los Angeles Street was changed to Anaheim Boulevard. Palm Street became Harbor Boulevard, while parts of Center Street and Chartres Street were changed to Lincoln Avenue.

# CHAPTER 18

Courtesy of the Anaheim History Room

# Orange Gold
# and Alligator Pears
## (1910–1920)

Citrus turned out to be Anaheim's most successful crop. The town became known as the center of the Valencia Orange District. Orange growers formed **cooperative groups** to sell their citrus crops. Colorful shipping crate labels were created to identify the fruit and where it came from. Boxes of citrus were shipped all over the country by 1910, with Anaheim labels on box ends.

Courtesy of Virginia Criss Geldman

*Criss Family Fruit Stand with the alligator sign on Los Angeles Street near Water Street and the old water tower.*

Courtesy of Virginia Criss Geldman

*Caligator Pears packing label on boxes.*

In 1910 a new variety of avocado was developed in Anaheim by E. C. Dutton. It was shaped like a pear, but much bigger. Some weighed over a pound and sold for a dollar each. They had green bumpy skin and people called them alligator pears. The end of the box they were shipped in read Caligator Pears from California.

The original name for this fruit was Ahuacate, which means avocado. Mr. Dutton named his variety the Anaheim avocado. A few Anaheim avocado trees can still be found in back yards around town.

Courtesy of the Anaheim History Room

*Sunkist packing house*

**Packing houses** were built next to railroad lines to make shipping the local fruit easy. The last and most modern packing house was built in 1917 by the Anaheim Orange & Lemon Association. Now known as the Sunkist Packing House, it still stands on the corner of Anaheim Boulevard and Santa Ana Street.

Courtesy of the Anaheim History Room

*A hose cart pulled by volunteer firefighters*

During Anaheim's early years, the Fire Department was located in the back of City Hall. Volunteer firemen received two dollars every time they helped fight a fire. When the bell at the firehouse sounded, volunteers rushed to help pull the hose cart to the fire.

William Duckworth owned the feed store next door to City Hall. He bought a delivery truck around

*William Duckworth with his delivery truck*

1912. After that, the city paid him two dollars to pull the hose cart to fires. Anaheim got its first motorized fire truck in 1915.

*Conrad "Cooney" Mauerhan driving Anaheim's first motorized fire truck decorated for the 4th of July parade*

In those days, everyone came to downtown Anaheim on Saturday nights. The stores all stayed open late. Men gathered at the barbershop or sporting

Courtesy of the Anaheim History Room

*Owners of the SQR Department Store, Schumacher and Renner*

goods stores. They talked about agricultural crops, hunting, or politics. Women liked to visit Falkenstein's Department Store and the SQR Store.

The children loved going to Fischle's Ice Cream Parlor and Candy Kitchen. The Fairyland Theater was

Courtesy of the Anaheim History Room

*Owner Richard Fischle behind the soda fountain at Fischle's Ice Cream Parlor*

a favorite, too. A new and bigger Fairyland Theater, with a balcony, was built in 1915. It showed silent movies on some nights and had live entertainment on other nights.

Every spring the orange blossoms in the groves surrounding Anaheim filled the air with the sweetest smell you could imagine. The groves were a perfect shady playground for local children once school was out. Those same groves with their orange and gold fruit kept Anaheim's economy growing.

# CHAPTER 19

Courtesy of the Anaheim History Room

# Rudy's Park
## (1920s)

The location for a city park was finally chosen in 1920. It was 20 acres, bordered by Palm Street on the west and Lemon Street on the east. Sycamore and Cypress streets were the north and south borders. The pioneer families of Dickel, Bullard, and Turck agreed to sell that land for $70,000. By 1927, Anaheim was known as "the city with the beautiful park." No other community in the county had a park as beautiful as this one.

On the west end was a lighted softball field with a grandstand for viewing games. An Olympic-sized heated pool, called the Plunge, and bath house were built in the center.

Courtesy of the Anaheim History Room

*City Park Plunge*

The tennis courts and picnic grounds were also popular spots. Peaceful lagoons filled with goldfish and lily pads stretched along the northern edge.

Courtesy of the Anaheim History Room

*The Lily Ponds*

An open-air, Greek-style theater was built on the east end facing Lemon Street. Concerts are still held each summer under the stars in the Greek Theater.

Courtesy of the Anaheim History Room

*The Greek Theater*

The Plunge was replaced by a modern swimming pool and bath house near the grandstands in later years. Anaheim kids still take lessons and learn to swim at the park every summer.

One person important to the park was Charles R. Boysen, but everyone called him "Rudy." He was put in charge of City Park in 1928 and spent the rest of his life building Anaheim parks. The cactus garden with its many rare specimens was a special project of Rudy's. Protected by an iron fence, it is still a favorite of park visitors.

*Courtesy of the Anaheim History Room*

*Building the Cactus Gardens*

The city honored Rudy by naming the park on State College Boulevard after him. That park is the one with the life-sized airplane.

*Helen Butler*

*Life-sized airplane at Boysen Park*

Before he came to Anaheim, Rudy discovered a special berry plant that produced very large fruit. During the 1930's he gave some "scraggly" samples to Walter Knott for his farm in Buena Park. That berry turned out to be such a successful crop that Mr. Knott named them the boysenberry, in Rudy's honor.

Courtesy of the First American Title Corporation

*Mr. and Mrs. Walter and Knott standing beside their 1920s auto in front of the original berry stand*

Mr. Knott built a theme park called Knott's Berry Farm on the land where those first boysenberries grew.

The city park has grown more beautiful over the years. It still remains a favorite place for recreation in Anaheim. In 1960, the name City Park was changed to Pearson Park to honor longtime Mayor Charles Pearson. Over his lifetime Mayor Pearson did a lot for the people of Anaheim. In 1911, when he was thirteen-years-old, he helped collect money to establish the Anaheim Family YMCA. Later, when he was mayor, he voted to bring Disneyland to the city. For many years Mayor Pearson was seen walking his basset hound Beauregard through City Park.

# CHAPTER 20

Courtesy of the Anaheim History Room

# All Aboard
## (1920s)

The Union Pacific railroad came to Anaheim in 1923. They built a beautiful Spanish-style depot on the east side of town next to the tracks on North Atchison Street. During the 1990s that depot was moved to South Atchison Street, restored, and is now used as a child care center.

In 1924, a group of businessmen started the Community Industrial Land Company. The Company bought 40 acres at North Olive and La Palma streets. They sold the land to companies that would move their business to Anaheim.

The city was also experiencing a building boom. New homes and commercial buildings were built all over town. The third City Hall was built on Center Street.

Courtesy of the Anaheim History Room

*Anaheim's third city hall*

The city's first **skyscraper** was completed right across the street at 201 East Center Street. In 1924, it was the tallest building in Orange County at six-stories. It was called the Kraemer Building in honor of its first owner. When the building was new, a bank was on the first floor. Doctors and lawyers offices were on the upper floors. During the last renovation, those offices were changed into apartments.

Courtesy of the Anaheim History Room

*Kraemer Building, future building of American Savings Bank of Anaheim*

The 1920s downtown shopping district included five banks and a large new SQR Department Store.

*Six-story Kruemer Building*

The SQR Store was known by everyone to have the latest and best styles in all of Orange County. Their windows along the street always displayed the latest fashions sold in the store.

During this time, the city's population doubled in only three years, from just over 6,000 people to 12,500 people. A new business district called Five Points was built near the old west gate to the city. It served the growing population on that side of town.

*The SQR Department Store windows*

Good times and big growth in Anaheim seemed endless until the **stock market** crashed in October 1929. Because the biggest business in town was agriculture, Anaheim was not hit as hard as bigger cities.

# CHAPTER 21

# Parades and Ghosts in the Park
## (1920s)

When people study history, it is important to look at every part. Good lessons can be learned from both good and bad times.

This chapter tells about some of both—stories about heroes who helped change things in Anaheim, making it a better place for everyone.

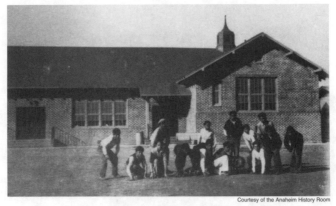

Courtesy of the Anaheim History Room

*Students in front of La Palma School*

In 1928, a new school was built north of town called the La Palma School. Latino children were required to attend that school. In the 1920s, many California communities had **segregated** schools. This meant there was one school for white children and a different one for non-white children. Before this time Anaheim's public schools were not segregated.

Schools in Anaheim were segregated for almost thirty years because some people thought children of

Courtesy of the Anaheim History Room

*La Palma School softball team, 1946*

different skin colors should not go to school together. When people learned it was wrong to have separate schools, the La Palma School was closed.

In 1950, the closed La Palma School was sold to Anaheim businessman Adolf Schoepe, the owner of

Courtesy of the Anaheim History Room

*La Palma Recreation Center, 1970*

Kwikset Lock Company. He became a local hero by turning the school into the La Palma Recreation Center where all children could play together. Other civic leaders joined him to make it a special place for everyone in the community to enjoy social activities.

The old school was home to many scout troops. Service clubs, like the Kiwanis and Lions clubs, also used the center. It became one of the most popular gathering places in town. Young people of all races used it until it was torn down in 1970 to make way for apartments.

On the evening of July 29, 1924, a crowd of 10,000 people jammed City Park. Many were dressed in white robes with hoods covering their heads so no one knew who they were. They looked like hooded ghosts.

Those men belonged to a secret organization called the **Ku Klux Klan**, or KKK. The members believed they were better than others who did not belong to their group. They tried to scare people by holding public rallies and lighting fires on people's front lawns.

Courtesy of the Anaheim History Room

*Lotus "Guv" Loudon*

After that big rally at City Park, Lotus Loudon, the owner of the Anaheim Bulletin newspaper, became a hero. Friends all called him "Guv." He wrote editorials against the KKK. He also published the secret membership list in his newspaper.

People were surprised to learn that many of the elected city leaders were members of that secret organization. After people found out, a special election was held in 1925. All the KKK members lost the election. Even some city employees who were members of the KKK resigned in disgrace.

Thanks to that courageous newspaper publisher, Anaheim was a nicer place for everyone to live without the secret organization of hooded ghosts.

The Anaheim Halloween Parade started around that same time. Guv Loudon was one of the founders. He said, "Ghosts marching in this parade are a far better use for bed sheets than the KKK rallies."

Courtesy of the Anaheim History Room

*Clown leading Halloween parade, 1946*

Now, more people understand how important it is to enjoy what is different about each other. Today's students learn about many cultures and what makes them special.

Courtesy of the Anaheim History Room

*Elephant "ghost" in Halloween parade, 2006*

# CHAPTER 22

# Shaking and Floating Houses
## (1930–1940)

After the stock market crashed in 1929, the **Great Depression** followed. Banks closed and many people lost their savings. Everyone was affected when people had no money and some people lost their jobs. Without money to buy things, people in Anaheim relied on their gardens and livestock for food.

Marion Wisser Harvey recalled that "the depression was a scary time that affected everyone." Her dad owned a sporting goods store downtown. One day, he earned only one dime for fixing a flat tire on a bike. She said that "living in a small town where everyone knew everyone and friends helped friends somehow made it easier."

*1939 earthquake damages many buildings*

Around dinner time on March 10, 1933, the first shock of an earthquake hit. Rose Hargrove Deneau was a young girl. She remembered the floor began to jump up and down in her grandma's kitchen. Her grandma yelled, "It's an earthquake! Get out of the house!"

The family was okay, but the children were not allowed to sleep in the house that night. They spent the night in the car. It rocked with every aftershock.

Four people in the county died from injuries caused by the earthquake. No one in Anaheim was killed.

Many buildings were damaged. Some had to be torn down because they were unsafe. The beautiful old 1912 Anaheim High School building was one of them. That disaster resulted in better **building codes**

*Courtesy of the Anaheim History Room*

*Anaheim High School building unsafe after the 1933 earthquake*

to make sure buildings would be safe if there was another earthquake.

Anaheim is located on a portion of the Santa Ana River that flooded easily. Because of that, it was

*Courtesy of the Anaheim History Room*

*Aerial view of 1938 flood*

flooded many times over the years between 1862 and 1969. The biggest and most famous flood came on the morning of March 3, 1938. It rained 22 inches in 48 hours.

Upstream from Anaheim, the riverbanks overflowed and water flooded both sides. The water was rushing so fast it swept everything in its way downstream. One couple rode down the river on the roof of their house for five miles to Anaheim.

The Japanese settlement near the northwest city limits was completely washed away. Water covered every part of the city. It was between six- and eight-feet deep in some places.

Courtesy of the Anaheim History Room

*Looking down Los Angeles Street from Center Street in the flood*

Communication with the world was cut off. The military came to patrol the streets and help the police.

Courtesy of the Anaheim History Room

*National Guard patrols the streets after the flood*

Houses were moved off their foundations. Cars and even large trucks floated along the river. Many people from Anaheim and the surrounding area lost their lives.

Courtesy of the Anaheim History Room

*House after the flood*

Flood damages cost the city millions of dollars. That disaster led to the construction of the Prado Dam, near Corona, to prevent floods from happening.

# CHAPTER 23

Courtesy of the Anaheim History Room

# Victory Gardens
## (1941–1947)

After the United States entered World War II, many changes happened in Anaheim. Troops and army equipment were familiar sights passing through town. Many men and women from Anaheim joined the military.

Courtesy of the Anaheim History Room

*Francis Patin, Jr.*

Blackout curtains, gas ration cards, and victory gardens became part of life in Anaheim. Blackout

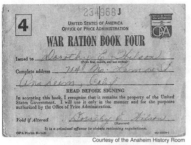
Courtesy of the Anaheim History Room

*Ration card used during the war*

curtains were made of black paper or cloth. They were put over the windows at night to block the light in case enemy airplanes flew over.

Gasoline was needed to win the war, so the government limited how much people could buy. Everyone needed a gas ration card to buy gas.

People were also asked to plant a vegetable garden to make sure there was enough extra food for the troops.

It was a way everyone could help win the victory, which is why everyone called them victory gardens.

Courtesy of the Anaheim History Room

*Victory gardens in Anaheim*

Courtesy of the Anaheim History Room

*Women working in packing houses during the war*

While men were away fighting the war, women went to work in packing houses and factories, making everything from parachutes to airplanes. The Dinkel sisters still tell stories about those days. During the war they worked in an aircraft factory west of town, building planes. The space inside the wings was very small. The smallest sister got to crawl into the wings to put fasteners on the inside.

Agriculture was Anaheim's biggest business in 1942. That year, the U.S. signed the Bracero Farm Worker agreement with Mexico. It allowed braceros to legally enter the United States. Bracero was the name given to those Mexican farm workers who came to the United States to work on farms under that government agreement. It was a time when American farms needed workers to replace the men who were away fighting the war.

After the Japanese attack on Pearl Harbor in Hawaii, the government was afraid some Japanese residents living in the U.S. might be spying for Japan. They sent all the Japanese American residents to camps were they could be watched until the war ended. That included all of Anaheim's Japanese American farmers, which provided even more work for the braceros.

Courtesy of the Anaheim History Room

*Heart Mountain Internment Camp Camera Club, 1942*

Courtesy of the Anaheim History Room

*Smudge pots keep the orchards from freezing*

An important source of news in the 1940s was the radio. Farmers listened each night for the latest weather forecast. It told them when they needed to fire up the smudge pots in winter. Smudge pots were metal containers with smoke stacks. They held oil for burning on cold nights.

*Frozen trees covered with icicles*

They used the smudge pots to keep the orchards warm and the oranges from freezing overnight. The burning oil also created a thick, black smoke that filled the air. A thick, oily black dust covered everything and everyone around the orchards.

News was not the only reason families loved their radios. Regular radio shows entertained the whole family. One of the most popular radio show celebrities was Jack Benny. One night in 1945, his radio announcer shouted, "Train leaving on track five for Anaheim, Azusa, and Cucamonga." Everyone laughed at the funny-sounding names. That announcement became a regular part of his show.

*Jack Benny visits in Anaheim, 1947*

Mr. Benny appeared at Anaheim's Civic Progress Week in 1947. He was given keys to the city and made the Honorary Mayor of Anaheim. Many people remember hearing him talk on the radio about being the "mayor" of Anaheim.

# CHAPTER 24

Courtesy of the Anaheim History Room

# Freeways and People Come to Town
## 1946–1964

The next big population growth for Anaheim began when World War II ended. Soldiers returning home wanted to start families and they needed houses. Many of Anaheim's orange groves were quickly turned into Anaheim's first housing tracts.

Anaheim's location in the middle of orange groves was always attractive to people from cold climates.

Many military men remembered the charming, small town they passed through during the war and came back.

Growing **industries**, like the **aerospace** factories, needed more workers. By the end of the 1940s, Anaheim's population was almost 15,000 people.

*Nortronics Corp, a division of Northrop Corp.*

In the early 50s the first freeway was built south from Los Angles following the railroad route through Anaheim. Before the freeway a trip to Anaheim took hours on a maze of streets. Using the new freeway it was only 45 minutes. That meant it was easier for new industries and people to come to Anaheim.

During the 1950s, it was quick and easy to **annex** land. Annexing is a way to add land and expand a city. Most of the farmland east and west of the city was added in that way. Anaheim was adding people and land so fast that it became the fastest growing city in the United States. Agriculture was no longer Anaheim's main industry. Aerospace, construction, and tourism replaced the farms as the places most people worked.

In October 1955, the Anaheim Shopping Center, now called Anaheim Plaza, opened on Euclid Street at the 5 freeway. It was the first

*Aerial view of Anaheim Plaza*

shopping mall in Orange County. The new Broadway Store located there was the largest department store in the county.

The whole town celebrated Anaheim's 100th birthday in 1957. The population reached 70,000 people that year. A big **Centennial** celebration was held that September. The main event was a play called *Centurama*, which told the story of Anaheim's history. Each night for a week crowds filled the stadium at La Palma Park. They watched a cast of 1,200 residents telling Anaheim's story.

*Ladies dress for Centurama*

*Keystone Kops celebrate the Centennial*

By that time, the city had outgrown all of its civic buildings. The first modern city building approved by voters was the library which was built in 1963 at Broadway and Palm Street (now Harbor Boulevard).

Former police Chief Jimmie Kennedy remembers when he was a detective in the old police station at City Hall. A call came in from the bank across the street in the Kreamer building saying it was being robbed. It was summer and the windows were open so they jumped out the closest window, ran across the street and caught the bank robbers before they got away.

Courtesy of Jimmie Kennedy

*Old police station in the back of City Hall early 1960s windows in the middle are the ones police jumped out*

The old police station at city hall had only two jail cells, so more room was needed. A new police station was built next door to the Library on Harbor Boulevard in 1964.

Courtesy of the Anaheim History Room

*New Police Station, 1964*

The small town of Anaheim had grown up in both size and population. It was a big city of almost 200,000 people as the 1960s ended.

# CHAPTER 25

Courtesy of the Anaheim History Room

# A Mouse Comes to Anaheim
## (July 17, 1955)

By 1950, Walt Disney was already known for the creation of Mickey Mouse and movies like *Snow White*. Around that time artists from his studio volunteered to help design floats for Anaheim's annual Halloween parade. The parade was a very big deal in town at that time.

Courtesy of the Anaheim History Room

*Mickey and Minnie Mouse in an early Halloween parade*

Around that same time, Walt Disney was dreaming of a new kind of amusement park. It would be a clean, safe, very special place for families to enjoy all year round. He wanted to build it near the Disney Studio in Burbank. The city of Burbank did not like his idea and said no. Amusement parks were thought to be dirty, rowdy places. They did not want one in their city.

Courtesy of the Anaheim History Room

*Walt Disney*

A study was done to figure out the best place to build Walt's dream park. The study said Anaheim was in the right location. Anaheim was a small town with friendly people and it reminded Walt of Marceline, Missouri, where he grew up. Would people in Anaheim like his idea? Anaheim's leaders saw that Disney's dream park was different from other amusement parks. It was full of new ideas.

Courtesy of the Anaheim History Room

*Construction begins at the site of Disneyland*

Walt promised the mayor it would be a family place that was always clean and that the park would be a good neighbor. The plans were announced in 1954. After that, people knew Anaheim as the home of Disneyland. One hundred and sixty acres of orange groves south of downtown was selected and construction began.

Courtesy of the Anaheim History Room

*Walt Disney, host of the Disneyland Show*

That same year, a weekly television show started on the ABC national network. It was called the *Disneyland Show*. Families all over the country watched it on Sunday nights. Walt began each show with a progress report on the park. Kids in every state watched as the park was built. They all dreamed of coming to Anaheim, California for a day at the Disneyland park when it opened.

*Disneyland under construction*

It was a race to complete the park on time. The gates opened on July 17, 1955. Millions of people watched celebrity host Art Linkletter tour the park live on TV. More than 28,000 people showed up that Sunday. That was a lot more than they expected.

*Mickey Mouse Club Mouseketeers in Opening Day Parade*

Some people even climbed fences to sneak in. It was so hot that ladies' high heeled shoes made dents in the new pavement. Drinking fountains didn't work and some rides broke down.

Walt wondered if he had made a big mistake! Was the park doomed like critics said? In just seven weeks, the one millionth guest entered Disneyland's Main Street, U.S.A. Disneyland was in Anaheim to stay.

Anaheim native Margaret Peters remembers taking a busload of Anaheim Sunday school children as invited guests to the park on opening day. For many years after that, Disneyland invited her "kids," as Margaret called them, to attend special events.

After Disneyland's opening, many tourists began arriving in Anaheim. Hotels and motels sprang up along the streets around the park. That was the

Courtesy of the Anaheim History Room

*Disneyland surrounded by orange grove – now the Resort District*

135

beginning of what is now called the Resort District on the south side of town.

One of the best parts about going to Disneyland is still the fireworks show. Many Anaheim residents can see the fireworks from their houses. Generations of Anaheim children have grown up with the memory of Disneyland's summer fireworks.

# CHAPTER 26

# City Government
## (1950s–1960s)

From Anaheim's beginning as an agricultural town, growth was slow and steady for almost 100 years. The big changes in the 1950s changed the little farm town forever. New jobs and houses attracted more people than ever before.

In 1957, houses were built everywhere. Anaheim became a modern-day boom town. People moved to Anaheim by the hundreds. The city continued to grow in size by annexing land from the farms of West

*City Hall, 1923*

Anaheim. In just two years, the city grew four times bigger. That set the pattern of growth for the future.

Notice Anaheim's uneven shape on the modern map compared to the square of the original colony. A former city councilwoman, Shirley McCracken, tells the story of how that happened. "During the 1950s, a **developer** would check with all the cities bordering his land to find out how much the city would charge him for services like sewer and water. Then, he would ask that his land be annexed to the city that gave him the best deal. Sometimes the land next to his, or even across the road, was annexed to another city. That is why the boundary lines of modern Anaheim look like they do.

Anaheim was growing so fast that changes were needed. A new city **charter** was written and a document called a **general plan**, which balanced city growth, was adopted in 1963. In 1964, voters adopted a charter form of government. The charter allowed the city to be more independent from the state government.

Under the charter form of government, the city had five elected city council members. They were all elected **at large**. That means a city council person could live anywhere in the city. He, or she, was elected by a majority of voters from the whole city. City council members then voted to elect one of them the mayor.

The biggest change made since that time was in 1974. Voters decided they wanted to elect their mayor separately from the city council. The city council still has five members. Four council members and the mayor are each elected by citizens from the whole city.

The city council votes on how money is spent and on laws that make the city safe and a good place to live. They give direction to the city manager who runs the city like a business manager. In 1966, the city council voted for a bed tax to help raise money for the construction of the Anaheim Convention Center.

Courtesy of the Anaheim History Room

*City council meeting, 1959*

When people stay at a hotel they are renting that bed for the nights they use it. Before they pay for the room, an extra tax is added to their total bill. That is how it came to be called a bed tax. Money from the bed tax is used to help the city provide services to the visitors and its residents. The amount of the bed tax has been raised over the years to keep providing good city services for everyone.

# CHAPTER 27

Courtesy of the Anaheim History Room

# Tamales and Tin Shops
## (1870–2006)

Immigrants with big dreams have been coming to Anaheim ever since 1857. They dreamed in many languages as they learned English together. Two of the businesses started by immigrants in the 1800s continued in Anaheim for over 100 years.

The oldest one was founded around 1870 by Joseph Bennerscheidt, a German tinsmith. He made buckets and other metal containers in his tin shop. After Joseph's death in 1921, the business was carried on by Joseph's son and grandson as the Benner Sheet Metal Works.

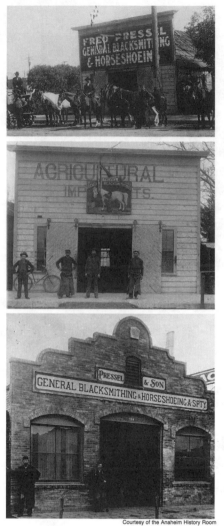

Courtesy of the Anaheim History Room

*Pressel's Blacksmith Shops, 1895-1910, 1900, 1913 (top to bottom)*

In 1894, Fred Pressel started a stable and blacksmith shop on Center Street. That was a good business to start when everyone traveled by horse and buggy. The Pressel family changed their business into a machine shop when machines replaced horses. The family name was kept on the business. The Pressel family also preserved the last orange grove in the old city on Santa Ana Street.

Small grocery markets were in most neighborhoods by the early 1900s. New immigrants owned and operated many of them. Anton's Food Market, on the corner of Los Angeles and Lemon Streets, was one

of them. Another was the
North Gate Market where
the Gonzales family chain
started. Many small
businesses used their family
name, like Anton's and Alex's
Tamales.

Courtesy of the Anaheim History Room

*Anton's Market*

By the late 1940s, a dozen Syrian-Lebanese
families had settled in Anaheim. Those families have
been joined by others from many Middle Eastern
countries. Over the years a large Arab business district
developed along a section of Brookhurst Street in
Anaheim.

One Italian immigrant
began collecting trash from
homes in Anaheim
neighborhoods during the
1930s. That was before cities
provided regular trash or
garbage collection. With a
desire to be successful and
with lots of hard work,
Cosmos V. (Dick) Taormina

Courtesy of the Anaheim History Room

*Dick Taormina and
his trucks*

started his trash-hauling business with an old Chevy
pickup truck.

In 1949, he officially founded the Anaheim
Disposal Company. By the early 1990s, it grew into

Taormina Industries, the largest trash disposal company in Southern California. Other members of the Taormina family have started, or owned, other Anaheim businesses.

Do you know what famous hamburgers got their start in Anaheim? Restaurants that serve them are named after the founder. That's

right! Carl's Jr. started in Anaheim. In 1945, Carl and Margaret Karcher opened their first hamburger stand on north Palm Street. A Carl's Jr. is still near that spot. The street next to it was re-named Karcher Way, to honor Carl.

Courtesy of the Anaheim History Room

*Carl Karcher*

Courtesy of the Anaheim History Room

*The first Carl's Jr. opens in Anaheim, 1945*

Anaheim's business signs are in many languages. They reflect the languages spoken in Anaheim's homes and schools. People from all over the world still come to Anaheim with dreams of starting a business.

# CHAPTER 28

Courtesy of the Anaheim History Room

# Big Dreams and Big Events
## (1875–1960s)

Big dreams, ideas, and events have always found a home in Anaheim. The first was the dream of growing grapes and making wine in 1857.

Many big things happened first in Anaheim like the first trade show. It was an event called the California Valencia Orange Show. President Warren G. Harding opened the first one by telephone on May 17, 1921.

Three giant tents for exhibits and entertainment were setup on the spot where La Palma Park is today.

Courtesy of the Anaheim History Room

*Orange Show arch under construction and completed*

By 1926, over 70,000 visitors passed through the arched three story high entrance. The last California Valencia Orange Show was held in 1931.

Courtesy of the Dutton Family

*The Jungle Gardens*

The first tourist attraction in Anaheim after World War II was the Jungle Gardens. It opened three years before Disneyland. **Exotic** birds in more than 500 palm trees looked down on pools filled with alligators. There was even an elephant named Anaheim, everyone called her Anna.

The star attraction was a **chimpanzee** named Jerry. He was dressed in little boy clothes and called "the world's most human chimpanzee." Sometimes he sneaked into the Jungle Gardens restaurant to enjoy rum soaked pineapples and a cigar! Then the manager had to call Jerry's owner Jack Dutton to come get him.

Courtesy of the Dutton Family

*Jerry the chimp*

Jack Dutton was the son of E.C. Dutton who developed the Anaheim avocado while Jack was growing up in Anaheim. In 1970 Jack Dutton became the 35th Mayor of Anaheim and served the city for four years as the Mayor.

Courtesy of the Dutton Family

*Mayor Dutton*

In 1961, a group of Anaheim businessmen with big dreams organized the Anaheim Visitor and Convention Bureau. They talked city leaders into building the Anaheim Convention Center on Katella Avenue.

Courtesy of the Anaheim History Room

*The original Anaheim Convention Center*

*Goofy, Mickey and Pluto visit the Anaheim Convention Center*

A big convention center next door to family entertainment like Disneyland was a new idea. The ground breaking began with a big dynamite blast. An arena designed to look like something from outer space that would seat over 9,000 people was built first. Opening week in July 1967 was celebrated with a special big event each night. Concerts, boxing, and even ballet drew big crowds.

The Anaheim Convention Center was a huge success! It has been expanded many times since then.

*The New Anaheim Convention Center, 2005*

Large trade shows every year bring millions of new visitors to Anaheim from all over the world.

*Signed photo of Ronald Reagan with 10 year old Paul and his parents Eleanor and Dr. William Kott.*

A future president was part of another big event. In 1966, movie actor, Ronald Reagan kicked off his 1st campaign for election as California Governor in Anaheim. That event was held at the home of Dr. and Mrs. William Kott. Mr. Reagan was quoted in the Anaheim Bulletin as telling the story, "I received the coldest reception ever when directed by Mrs. Kott to the powder room where I found the toilet filled with ice cubes." Earlier, unknown to the hostess, the ice had been dumped there by a busboy. Reagan was elected governor of California later that year and again in 1970. He went on to become the 40th president of the United States in 1981 and served two terms as president.

Courtesy of the Anaheim History Room

*Anaheim Stadium, 1966*

Courtesy of the Anaheim History Room

*Motocross events held at Anaheim Stadium*

Another big dream in 1965 was building a stadium for Major League Baseball. Since opening in 1966 the stadium has been used for more than baseball. Big crowds are also attracted there for motocross, religious crusades and even rock concerts.

All those things gave people more reasons to visit Anaheim, and the city kept growing.

# CHAPTER 29

Courtesy of Anaheim History Room

# Anaheim Goes Major League
## (1960–2008)

Watching baseball was always a favorite Anaheim pastime. The first baseball team with a big "A" on their jerseys played ball in Anaheim during the 1890s.

Courtesy of the Anaheim History Room

*Grandstand at City Park*

During 1939, baseball great Connie Mack and the Philadelphia Athletics came to Anaheim for spring training. A new stadium was built for those games at La Palma Park. The whole town came out to watch professional baseball that spring.

Courtesy of the Anaheim History Room

*Spring Training at La Palma Park, 1939*

Courtesy of the Anaheim History Room

*California pennant held by owner Gene Autry*

In the 1960s, cowboy singer and baseball owner Gene Autry was looking for a new home field for his California Angels baseball team. Rex Coons was Anaheim's mayor and a baseball fan.

The mayor convinced other city leaders that Anaheim should build a baseball stadium. The California Angels began playing in Anaheim Stadium on opening day of the 1966 season. The stadium was nick-named the "Big A" that year.

In 1978 the Los Angeles Rams decided to move to the Big A, but they needed more seats. The Big A scoreboard was moved to the parking lot and the stadium was enclosed to add more seats. The Rams played football at Anaheim Stadium until 1994, when the owner decided to move the team to her home town, St. Louis. The team became the St. Louis Rams.

*Courtesy of the Anaheim History Room*

*Gene Autry in front of the Big A under construction*

The Big A stadium was again remodeled when The Walt Disney Company purchased an interest in the Angels in 1995. The stadium was turned back into a baseball-only style park with an open outfield. All of Anaheim cheered as the Anaheim Angels won their first World Series there in 2002.

*Courtesy of the Anaheim History Room*

*Anaheim Stadium fully enclosed, 1980*

Another part of Anaheim and Big A history are All-star baseball games, postseason football **bowl games**, and baseball playoffs.

City leaders were not yet done building beautiful places for sporting events. Next was the Anaheim

153

**Arena** in the 1990s. It was first known as the Arrowhead Pond, home of the Mighty Ducks NHL professional hockey team. In addition to **Stanley Cup** hockey playoffs, other world championship events have been held at the Pond.

Courtesy of the Anaheim History Room

*The Arrowhead Pond, later changed to the Honda Center*

Renamed the Honda Center in 2006, it is still the home ice for Anaheim Ducks hockey. On June 6, 2007, the Ducks became the first California team ever to win the championship Stanley Cup. They celebrated with a big party for their fans at the Honda Center.

Courtesy of the Anaheim Ducks

*Championship Ducks with the Stanley Cup*

The Honda Center is also known all over the world as one of the best places in the United States to attend a music concert.

# CHAPTER 30

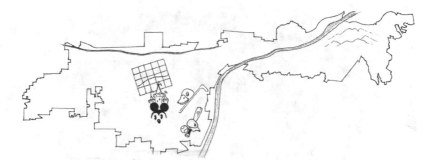

# Anaheim's Size and Shape Changes
## (1970–1990)

Anaheim's boundaries were about to change one more time. This time the hills southeast of the river to the Riverside County line were annexed. Now Anaheim covered almost 50 square miles, from the eastern hills to the flat land in West Anaheim. Anaheim's next housing boom was ready to happen in

Courtesy of the Anaheim History Room

*Some of the first houses in Anaheim Hills*

the hills. That new section of the city became known as Anaheim Hills.

Courtesy of the Anaheim History Room

*Orange County's first mall, Anaheim Plaza*

By the 1970s, malls had replaced old downtowns as community gathering spots. Local residents no longer went downtown to shop. It was clear Anaheim's

Courtesy of the Anaheim History Room

*Old downtown Anaheim*

old downtown near City Hall needed improvement. **Redevelopment** was introduced as a tool government could use to fix up old, run-down sections of the city.

Anaheim's first redevelopment project was created in 1972 and was called Project Alpha. It included the

old downtown
and the
Canyon
Industrial
Area, which
runs along La
Palma Avenue
and the
Santa Ana

Courtesy of the Anaheim History Room

*Bulldozer in old downtown*

River. Leaders thought the only way to **revitalize** a
city was to bulldoze every old building, then replace
them with new, modern buildings.

There were lots of ideas for what should replace
Anaheim's old downtown. Some leaders wanted hotels
and tourist attractions. A man-made lake was even
considered.

Many people were afraid everyone would forget
the city's history when buildings were demolished.
The Anaheim Historical Society was founded during
those years.
The Society
worked to
teach people

**Anaheim Historical Society, Inc.**

FOUNDED IN 1976

about Anaheim's history and save some of the old
buildings from the bulldozers.

Some old houses were saved. The best ones were
moved to new locations. But most of the old civic and

Courtesy of the Anaheim History Room

*The Benner house moves down a city street to it's new location*

commercial buildings were torn down. The whole block behind the old City Hall was cleared to build a new **Civic Center**.

Courtesy of the Anaheim History Room

*New City Hall and Civic Center*

A new seven-story City Hall was the first building on that site. It was Anaheim's fourth City Hall and opened in 1980. That changed the look of Anaheim's old downtown again.

# CHAPTER 31

Courtesy of the Placentia History Room

# Rebuilding in Old Anaheim
## (1980–2000)

It was many years before the last downtown building was finally bulldozed during the 1980s. Many more years passed before building on the vacant land started.

What people thought Anaheim's new downtown should look like was changing. A new downtown began to take shape. It grew slowly and in stages over the years, much like the original downtown did.

*Anna's Home by the River*

Courtesy of the Anaheim History Room

*New City Hall West*

An 11-story high-rise building called City Hall West was completed in November 1992. It was built as a home for the Anaheim Public Utilities, which is still owned by the citizens of Anaheim. The building also provides a home for other city departments.

Another high-rise office building was built for the telephone company. Two large parking structures and spaces for stores were also built along the new street, named Center Street Promenade.

The Walt Disney Company built a gleaming, silver ice rink in downtown. Designed by Frank Geary as the practice rink for the Ducks Hockey team, it can

Courtesy of the Anaheim History Room

*Ducks' hockey ice rink downtown*

160

even be seen from outer space. Anaheim kids learn to ice skate and play hockey there, too.

Some old buildings, like the Kraemer Building and Carnegie Library, were restored and **adapted** for new uses.

In the early 2000s, new buildings were built with features inspired by the old downtown of the 1920s. Anaheim's old downtown continues to be a mix of old and new. The two City Halls stand on each side of Anaheim Boulevard at the historic center of the city.

Courtesy of the Anaheim History Room

*Kwikset Lock Co., 1960s*

Some businesses, like Kwikset Locks, have left Anaheim. Their old industrial buildings were bulldozed. New homes and parks are replacing them. The Rockwell Corporation helped put the first men into space with technology developed in Anaheim. In the 1990s, they merged with Boeing Aircraft Company.

In 1991, the Walt Disney Company announced they wanted to build a second theme park on their parking lot. Building a new park next to Disneyland sparked changes during the 1990s. City leaders and the Walt Disney Company dreamed of changing the **hodge-podge** of businesses and signs along the streets into a beautiful garden district.

*Resort district, before and after*

Courtesy of the Anaheim History Room

Everyone worked together on a plan to do that. The result is the beautiful palm lined streets of the Resort District in the city. At the same time, bulldozers went to work on a new park, known as Disney's California Adventure Park, next to Disneyland in the center of the Resort District.

# CHAPTER 32

Courtesy of the City of Anaheim

# Preserving Anaheim History
## (1990–2007)

As the 20th century came to an end the old town site was busy with activity. Old houses were moved and restored. They were fixed up to look like they did when they were new, not like a modern house. Neighborhoods of new houses were built to look like old styles on land that had been cleared. An apartment village was created next to a neighborhood of old houses near downtown.

Citrus Park was built on South Atchison Street. The original Union Pacific Depot was restored next to the park. That was on an old industrial land near the railroad tracks. Now Atchison Street looks like streets did in the 1920s, lined with old houses.

Attracted by interesting old houses, many new people moved to the old part of Anaheim. Homeowners worked with the city to create a historic district. The City Council liked that idea and officially recognized the first historic district in October 1997. It is called The Colony Historic

District. The boundaries are where the willow fence was around the original Anaheim colony. Monuments now mark the places where the original gates kept the cattle out.

Beautiful old houses can be seen along most of the original city streets in the Colony. Hundreds of owners have learned

Courtesy of the Anaheim History Room

*Anaheim Colony Historic District*

the history of their homes. Many can tell you stories about who built their house and who lived there before them.

New parks in old neighborhoods were built. One of them is on the site of the original Central School. It is named George Washington Park after the school it replaced. With a **gazebo** and a long **rose arbor**, it looks like parks did in the early 1900s.

*George Washington Park*

In 2004, the Five Points Historic District on the west side was approved. The third historic district

Gail Eastman

*The Dieham "catalog" house, built in 1924*

directly north of the Colony was approved in 2006. It is called The Historic Palm District. Work is continuing to identify historic homes and buildings all over the city. Old buildings and places help everyone to connect with Anaheim's history.

Courtesy of the Anaheim History Room

*Woelke family in front yard of*
*their Victorian home*

A group called the Mother Colony Household worked with the city to preserve the first house built in Anaheim. In 2006, the city purchased the Victorian Woelke-Stoffel house and the land next to the Mother Colony House on West Street. The houses will be preserved as a part of Anaheim's history in a small historic park.

The Anaheim Historical Society presents programs to teach people about Anaheim history. The Society also supports local historic preservation and holds public tours of Anaheim's old houses.

Another good place to learn more about Anaheim's history is the Heritage Reading Room of the library at the Muzeo. The history room makes Anaheim's history available to everyone. A part of their collection of historic photos can be viewed on the Internet. They can be found by going to the city's website at www.anaheim.net.

# CHAPTER 33

Courtesy of the Anaheim History Room

# Celebrities Who Called
# Anaheim Home
## (1876–2009)

Anaheim may be best known to the world as the home of Disneyland and Mickey Mouse. Even before Mickey came to town, many famous people, or celebrities, called Anaheim home.

Music and art were important to the settlers. Many Anaheim pioneers were musicians, artists, or writers. The first public buildings built in the city were a school and an opera house.

Madame Helena Modjeska, the famous Polish actress, was Anaheim's first celebrity. Her statue is in Pearson Park near the theater. She is dressed as Mary, Queen of Scots, from her favorite stage role.

Courtesy of the Anaheim History Room

*Madame Helena Modjeska*

A friend of hers, and fellow Polish immigrant, was writer Henryk Sienkiewicz. After seeing a traveling French circus in Anaheim, he wrote a play called *Orso*. It tells the story of a circus weightlifter who falls in love with a female acrobat. He wrote *Quo Vadis*, a novel about religious **persecution**, which received the Nobel Prize for literature in 1905.

Courtesy of the Anaheim History Room

*Brian Downing, Anaheim resident and Angel baseball player*

Many people who went to school in Anaheim have become famous through the careers they chose. Several major league baseball players graduated from high schools in Anaheim. Some even played baseball for the Angels, like Brian Downing who graduated from Magnolia High School.

168

Courtesy of the Anaheim History Room

*Tiger Woods Learning Center*

Professional golfer Tiger Woods graduated from Western High School. He worked together with the city to build the Tiger Woods Learning Center, which opened in 2005. It is located next to Anaheim's Dad Miller Golf Course which was his home course while he was on the high school team.

Courtesy of the Anaheim History Room

*Bill Medley and Bobby Hatfield*

Bobby Hatfield graduated in Anaheim High's class of 1958. In the 1960s he and Bill Medley became famous singing together as The Righteous Brothers. They wrote and recorded many famous songs. One of their most famous love song was *Unchained Melody*.

Courtesy of the Anaheim History Room

*Gwen Stefani of No Doubt*

A girl from Loara High School's class of 1987, named Gwen Stefani, loved to sing. Her brother Eric wrote music. He teamed up with saxophonist Tony Kanal and a drummer Adrian Young to form a band. All four of them became celebrities in the 1990s as members of the underground band called "No Doubt." Gwen also went on to more fame and a successful solo career as a singer.

One of Anaheim's young teen celebrities was Lisa Tucker. She sang on the *American Idol* television program in 2006 while she was still a student at Kennedy High School.

Courtesy of the Anaheim History Room

*Lisa Tucker*

Many people who grew up in Anaheim have been elected to local, state and national public offices. Among the most recent ones are Loretta Sanchez who serves in the United States House of Representatives and State Senator Lou Correa. Anaheim has proved to be a good place to grow-up, attend school and develop your talents.

# CHAPTER 34

# New Dreams for Anaheim
## (2000–2007)

As the city entered the 21st century, it was time for an update of Anaheim's general plan. A city's general plan is a document that helps the leaders plan for the future. The new plan would create a vision or dream of what Anaheim would look like in the year 2030. All of Anaheim's residents were asked for ideas. Their ideas helped shape the plan to guide the city into the future.

People wanted to see more beautiful streets like those in the Resort District. They wanted safe neighborhoods and parks for their families. It was important to have new buildings with beautiful

Courtesy of the Anaheim History Room

*View of Platinum Triangle*

designs. Leaders encouraged each area of the city to continue developing its own special identity. Celebrating the differences is what makes Anaheim such a special city in which to live and work.

The area around Anaheim Stadium became known as The Platinum Triangle. New high-rise buildings were planned and built there. The vision for the Platinum Triangle was to create a new **urban-style** community.

Creating a transportation center for the county was another dream. It would be a place where people could leave their cars to ride on public transportation connecting them to any place in the world. The transportation station called ARTIC was planned for land near the stadium and the Santa Ana River.

Courtesy of the City of Anaheim

*ARTIC Transportation Center*

A large part of Irvine ranch land at the eastern
edge of Anaheim was planned for new homes, schools,
and parks. Named Mountain Park, it connects to
the beautiful open wilderness of the Cleveland
National Forest.

By the 1990s, much of the once beautiful Santa
Ana River bank was lined with concrete and barren
ponds. The trail along the banks was used mostly by
joggers and bicyclists.

City and community leaders worked on a plan to
change the river banks. A University of California
class even helped with ideas. The dream was to
transform sections of Anaheim along the Santa Ana
River and the ponds into beautiful and peaceful places
for people and wild life.

In 2006, Anaheim became the first large city in the
United States to establish a city-wide wireless internet
system in partnership with EarthLink.

Near City Hall,
new buildings
were built to fill
the empty spaces
in the old
downtown. The
Carnegie Plaza
Building behind

Courtesy of the Anaheim History Room

*Carnegie Plaza Building and*
*Carnegie Library*

Courtesy of the Anaheim History Room

*Carnegie Plaza Building, home of the Muzeo*

the old Carnegie Library was one of them.

The history room moved there in 2007. The new space linked the Carnegie Plaza Building to the old Carnegie Library. Together they became known as the Muzeo, creating a new home for traveling museum exhibits and cultural events in downtown Anaheim.

Those are just some of the new ideas and big dreams that began to take shape in the early years of the 21$^{st}$ century.

# CHAPTER 35

Always Fresh & Never Grows Old

City of Anaheim

# Happy 150th Birthday
## (2005–2007)

In 2005, Disneyland celebrated its 50th birthday with a big party that lasted more than a year. Anaheim's 150th birthday happened just two years later in 2007. It also lasted more than a year. The 150th birthday is called a **sesquicentennial**.

The sesquicentennial celebration started in the fall of 2006. A three-day Fall Festival with a revival of Anaheim's night time Halloween Parade was the kick-off event.

Courtesy of the Anaheim History Room

*Anaheim Sesquicentennial float*

"Always fresh never grows old" became the theme for Anaheim's celebration. A float in the 2007 Rose Parade in Pasadena announced to the world the start of Anaheim's birthday celebration. Everyone in Anaheim over 13-years-old was invited to help decorate the float during December. Anaheim students and residents were chosen to ride on the float in the parade on January 1, 2007.

The float was designed to be fun and to tell the whole world what a special place Anaheim is to live or visit.

A walk of fame was created on the sidewalk in the Resort District. The first star on the walk was for Walt Disney. Carl Karcher's star was the second.

A history walk was created and dedicated in June to honor Anaheim's history and pioneers. It is a part of the Muzeo, next to the historic Carnegie Library building in the heart of old downtown. The walk features a timeline, stories, and photos to make Anaheim's history come alive.

Special events were scheduled each month, including a giant birthday cake, a grand opening of the Imperial Rome exhibit at the Muzeo and much more. Not all the party plans were announced at one time. Some things were kept secret as surprises throughout the birthday year.

Gail Eastman

*Anaheim History Walk*

Many Anaheim residents remember how much fun they had celebrating the city's centennial birthday in 1957. Some of them helped plan the sesquicentennial celebration. Children who helped celebrated Anaheim's 150th birthday have their own stories to tell about the year long birthday party.

Anaheim history is filled with people who refused to give up. Even when they failed, they kept trying until they achieved their dreams. Anaheim has proved to be a good place to grow up, to follow dreams, to work hard, and to see those dreams come true. The next chapter of Anaheim's history will be as special and unique as the boys and girls who call Anaheim their home.

Anaheim children may become the next city leaders like those who founded the city and helped it grow. They may be the next dreamers like Walt Disney and Carl Karcher, whose fame stretches beyond Anaheim.

With hard work and belief in themselves every child's dream really can come true in Anaheim. Their accomplishments will be part of the history that we will celebrate at the 200th birthday party.

They may even get to help plan the next party to celebrate 200 years of Anaheim's history in 2057.

# Anaheim Facts

| | |
|---|---|
| **Incorporation Date** | February 10, 1870 |
| **City Motto** | Where the world comes to live, work and play |
| **City Tree** | Magnolia |
| **City Flower** | Calendula |
| **City Colors** | Blue and White |
| **Location** | Anaheim is located 28 miles southeast of Los Angeles and is the largest city in Orange County in terms of land. |
| **Size** | 50.5 square miles |
| **Elevation** | 160 feet |
| **Longitude** | 117.9055° |
| **Latitude** | 33.8323° |
| **Climate** | Average temperature 70 degrees |
| | Average annual rainfall 9.8 inches |
| **Population** | 2006 - 342,410 |
| | 2000 - 328,014 |
| | 1990 - 266,406 |
| | 1980 - 219,494 |
| | 1970 - 166,701 |
| | 1960 - 104,184 |
| | 1950 - 14,556 |
| | 1940 - 11,031 |
| | 1930 - 10,995 |
| | 1920 - 5,526 |
| | 1910 - 2,268 |
| | 1900 - 1,456 |
| | 1876 - 881 |
| **Median Age** | 32 years |

| | |
|---|---|
| **Education** | Public Schools serving Anaheim Students include:<br>  Elementary Schools  49<br>  Middle Schools 10<br>  High Schools  14 |
| **Libraries** | 5 (Central Library and 4 branch libraries) |
| **Parks** | 50<br>24 Neighborhood Parks<br>11 Community Parks<br>7 Mini-Parks<br>5 Nature Centers<br>3 Specialized Recreation Centers |
| **Employment** | 206,703 |
| **Largest Employers** | Walt Disney Resort<br>Kaiser Foundation Hospital<br>Boeing North America<br>Alstyle Apparel |

# Anaheim Mayors

From the Beginning of the City's Incorporation in
1870-1872 and 1876 to the Present

| | | |
|---|---|---|
| **Max Strobel**<br>1870 | **Max Nebelung**<br>1912–1913 | **Ralph B. Clark**<br>1969-1970 |
| **Henry Kroeger**<br>1871–1872 | **John H. Cook**<br>1914–1915 | **Jack C. Dutton**<br>1970–1974 |
| **John Fischer**<br>1876 | **John J. Dwyer**<br>1918–1919 | **William J. Thom**<br>1974–1978 |
| **Theodore Reiser**<br>1877, 1890–1891 | **William Stark**<br>1920–1923 | (first Mayor elected<br>by the citizens) |
| **Loring W. Kirby**<br>1878 | **Elmer H. Metcalf**<br>1924 | **John Seymour**<br>1978–1982 |
| **Benjamin F. Scibert**<br>1879–1880 | **Perry W. Mathis**<br>1925 | **Don Roth**<br>1982–1986 |
| **Benjamin Dreyfus**<br>1881–1882 | **Carl F. Leonard**<br>1926 | **Ben Bay**<br>1986–1988 |
| **John P. Zeyn**<br>1883 | **Walter L. Bigham**<br>1927 | **Fred Hunter**<br>1988–1992 |
| **Frederick A. Korn**<br>1884 | **Louis E. Miller**<br>1928–1931 | **Tom Daly**<br>1992–2002 |
| **Robert J. Northam**<br>1885–1886 | **Fred H. Koesel**<br>1932 | **Curt Pringle**<br>2002-Present |
| **Adolph Rimpau**<br>1887 | **Charles H. Mann**<br>1933-1940 | |
| **Frank Ey**<br>1888–1889 | **Charles A. Pearson**<br>1940–1959 | |
| **William A. Witte**<br>1892-1893 | **Adolph J. Schutte**<br>1959–1962 | |
| **Charles O. Rust**<br>1894–1899,<br>1904–1911 | **Rector L. Coons**<br>1962–1964 | |
| **Joseph Helmsen**<br>1900–1901 | **Odra L. Chandler**<br>1964–1965 | |
| **Julius J. Schneider**<br>1902 – 1903,<br>1916–1917 | **Fred T. Krein**<br>1965-1967 | |
| | **Calvin L. Pebley**<br>1967–1969 | |

# Timeline

1769 Don Gaspar de Portolà expedition passes through Orange County

1776 United States declares its independence on July 4th

1794 First concession of land from Spain is given to Manuel Nieto

1802 First concession of land from Mexico is given to Juan Pablo Grijalva and named El Rancho Santiago de Santa Ana

1821 Mexico wins independence from Spain and claims California

1834 Bernardo Yorba granted Rancho Canon de Santa Ana

1841 Ontiveros builds adobe home on ranch

1848 Gold is discovered in California at Sutter's Mill

1850 California becomes part of the United States as the 31st state

1854 First school in Orange County opens on the Yorba ranch

1855 A civil engineer, George Hansen, surveys the Ontiveros land and meets the Ontiveros family

1857 Ontiveros sells part of his ranch to George Hansen and the Vineyard Society, which becomes the city of Anaheim

1859 The Anaheim Water Company is formed to supply water to the vineyards

1860  Frederick W. Kuelp comes to Anaheim and opens the first public school

1860  The first child, Anna Fisher, is born in Anaheim

1862  Anaheim experiences its first great flood

1870  Anaheim incorporates and becomes The Town of Anaheim

1870  Joseph Bennerscheidt opens a roofing, tin, and plumbing business, which became Benner Sheet Metal Works, the oldest business in Anaheim

1875  The first railroad line, the Southern Pacific Railroad, reaches Anaheim

1876  Friedrich Conrad starts the first amusement park, Tivoli Gardens

1876  Madame Helena Modjeska arrives in Anaheim

1884  The grapes begin to die because of The Anaheim Disease and farmers turn to oranges and chili peppers

1888  The Santa Fe train depot is built

1889  County of Orange is formed by Governor Waterman

1895  Citizens vote to build a city-owned power generating plant, giving Anaheim electricity

1905  Anaheim author Henryk Sienkiewicz wins the Nobel Prize for *Quo Vadis*

1906  The Automobile Club of Southern California puts mission bells by the side of the road to mark the El Camino Real

1908  Andrew Carnegie gives Anaheim money to build its first public library

1910 Orange growers form cooperative groups and ship citrus all over the country

1914 World War I starts

1918 The Anaheim Orange and Lemon Growers Association Packing House is built

1920 The location for Anaheim's first city park is chosen

1921 California Valencia Orange Show opens

1924 The Ku Klux Klan holds a rally in City Park

1924 The city's first skyscraper, the Kraemer Building, is built

1928 Charles R. (Rudy) Boysen is put in charge of Anaheim's first park

1929 The stock market crashes, causing The Great Depression

1931 The last California Valencia Orange Show is held

1933 A great earthquake destroys buildings in Anaheim

1938 The biggest, most damaging flood hits Anaheim

1941 The United States enters World War II

1942 The United States signs the Bracero Farm worker agreement

1945 Carl and Margaret Karcher found Carl's Jr.

1949 Cosmo V. (Dick) Taormina founds Anaheim Disposal which became Taormina Industries

1952 Jack Dutton opens The Jungle Gardens

1953 Interstate 5 freeway to Anaheim is completed

1955 The Anaheim Shopping Center opens on Euclid Street

1955  Walt Disney builds a theme park, Disneyland

1961  Anaheim Visitor and Convention Bureau is organized

1963  Anaheim develops a general plan to help guide development

1964  Anaheim voters adopt a charter form of government

1966  City council creates the bed tax to raise money for the Anaheim Convention Center

1966  The California Angels, owned by Gene Autry, play their first season in Anaheim Stadium

1967  The Anaheim Convention Center opens

1972  Project Alpha, the first redevelopment project in Anaheim, begins

1972  Construction begins on the Anaheim Hills Planned Community

1974  Anaheim voters approved election of the mayor separate from city council

1980  Los Angeles Rams move to Anaheim

1980  Anaheim's fourth City Hall opens

1984  The Olympics are hosted in Los Angeles and the Anaheim Convention Center is used for two events

1987  The Anaheim Museum opens in the old Carnegie Library

1992  The Walt Disney Company opens a second theme park, Disney's California Adventure

1993  The Mighty Ducks hockey team started in Anaheim

1997  Anaheim's first historic district is officially recognized

2002  The Anaheim Angels win their first
      World Series
2005  Anaheim and Tiger Woods open the Tiger
      Woods Learning Center
2005  Disneyland celebrates its 50$^{th}$ anniversary
2006  Anaheim establishes a city-wide internet system
2007  Anaheim celebrates its 150$^{th}$ anniversary – the
      Anaheim Ducks hockey team wins the Stanley
      Cup championship
2008  U.S. Men's Volleyball team wins Olympic Gold
      Medal in China

# Glossary of Important Terms

**Aerospace** – Companies that build or design things used in space travel

**Abalone** – A type of shellfish

**Adapted** – Changed to make a better fit

**Adobe** – Brick made of clay and straw

**Annex** – To add or attach a small thing to a large thing

**Archaeologists** – A person who studies material from humans who lived long ago

**Arena** – A large structure that is used for sports or entertainment

**At-large** – A group that represents the whole city or state, not just a part of it

**Bacterium** – A group of one-celled organisms that can cause disease

**Boarding schools** – A school where children live away from their family

**Bowl games** – A special game played between two successful sports teams

**Brand** – A mark burned into cattle or livestock to indicate ownership

**Building codes** – Rules used to make buildings safe

**Catholicism** – Beliefs of Catholics

**Centennial** – Something that happens once every 100 years

**Charter** – A paper from the government that creates a business or a city

**Chimpanzee** – A large very smart ape or monkey

**Civic center** – A group of government buildings where government offices are

**Civil engineer** – A person who designs roads, bridges, sewers, or dams

**Concessions** – Government land given to someone in exchange for their agreement to use it in a certain way

**Constitution** – A document that establishes laws for a government

**Cooperative groups** – A group of people that work together for a common purpose

**County seat** – The town or city where government buildings for a county are located

**Delegates** – A person who acts a representative for a group of people

**Demolish** – To tear down something

**Developer** – A person who improves land to build new buildings or houses

**Drought** – A long period of time with little or no rain

**Editor** – A person who prepares and arranges newspapers or books

**Exotic** – Something that is from another part of the world

**Fib** – To tell a harmless lie

**Freight trains** – A train that transports goods or cargo, not people

**Gazebo** – A small roofed structure that is open on all sides

**General law city** – A city that is allowed to make its own laws

**General plan** – A city plan that guides officials in land uses and zones for future development

**Grant** – A paper that transfers property ownership from one person or group to another

**Great Depression** – The name given to a period of time in history from 1933 to 1939

**Hacienda** – A Spanish word, meaning a house on a large farm or ranch

**Hodge-podge** – A mix of many different things

**Ignoramus** – A person lacking in knowledge

**Immigrant** – A person who leaves one country and settles

permanently in another

**Industries** – A group of businesses that make or produce the same thing

**Invest** – To use money to buy something expecting to make more money

**Jerkins** – A close-fitting jacket or short coat, usually sleeveless

**Ku Klux Klan** – A club with secret membership of only white people. They persecuted other people because of their race or religion.

**Lance** – A long wooden pole with a pointed metal head, often used as a weapon

**Mill** – A building equipped with machinery for grinding grain into flour

**Mischievous** – Playful in a naughty or teasing way

**Mortar** – A bowl in which substances are crushed or ground with a pestle

**Packing houses** – An establishment for processing and packing foods

**Patriotism** – Great love for one's own country and loyalty to it

**Persecution** – To make someone suffer because of their race, religion or beliefs

**Pestle** – A tool for pounding or grinding substances in a mortar

**Porridge** – A cooked type of cereal

**Presidios** – A fort where soldiers live

**Rancho** – Spanish ranch

**Reatas** – A braided leather rope

**Redevelopment** – Rebuilding an area of a town or city that needs improvement

**Revitalize** – To make something new again

**Rose arbor** – A shaded sitting place or walk way covered by roses

**Saloon** – An old-fashioned bar

**Segregated** – To impose the separation of a race or class from the rest of society

**Sesquicentennial** – A 150ᵗʰ anniversary or its celebration

**Settlements** – Establishing a group of people in a new region

**Skyscraper** – A tall building with many stories

**Slaughtered** – The killing of animals especially for food

**Stanley Cup** – The championship trophy of the National Hockey League

**State legislature** – A person who makes laws for the state

**Stock market** – A place where stock and bond certificates are bought and sold

**Superintendent** – A person who oversees or directs work

**Survey** – To determine the boundaries of land by measuring angles and distances

**Trabuco rifle** – A type of rifle or gun

**Treaty** – An agreement between two individuals or groups

**Urban-style** – Tall buildings with people living upstairs and businesses along the street level floors.

**Vaqueros** – Spanish word meaning cowboy

**Vineyard** – A farm of grapevines where wine grapes are produced

**Windmill** – A machine that has wheels that run on the energy from wind

# Index

*Where to find special words.*

Karcher, 144, 178
Kate, 92, 93
Katella, 92, 93, 148
Kennedy, 170
Keystone Kops, 130
Kicha, 14
King Carlos, 20
Kiwanis, 111
KKK, 112
Knott, 103, 104
Kohler, 45, 46
Kraemer Building, 106, 107, 161
Kroeger, 92
Ku Klux Klan, 112
Kuchel, 52, 72
Kuelp, 59
Kwikset Lock, 111, 161
La Palma, 105, 110, 111, 130, 146, 152, 157
Langenberger, 36, 56, 60, 91, 92
Latino, 110
Leafhoppers, 77
Leather-jackets, 19, 21
Lemon, 69, 70, 96, 101, 102, 142
Lily Ponds, 102
Lincoln, Abraham, 62
Linkletter, 134
Loara, 62
Los Angeles, 14, 28, 36, 43, 45-48, 57, 69, 70, 72-74, 76, 84, 88, 89, 94, 118, 128, 142, 153
Loudon, 112
Major League Baseball, 149, 168
Manchester, 73
Marshall, 42
Mauerhan, 98
McCracken, 138
Medley, 169
Merchants, 67
Mexican, 35, 36, 41, 44, 123
Mickey Mouse, 131, 134, 167
Mickey Mouse Club Mouseketeers,

134
Mickle Backs, 86
Middle Eastern, 143
Mighty Ducks, 154
Mill, 42
Miller, 169
Miners, 43
Minnie Mouse, 132
Mission, 21, 28, 29, 31, 37, 55, 88
Missouri, 132
Modjeska, 75, 91, 168
Modjeska Canyon, 75
Monterey Bay, 20
Mother Colony, 47, 90, 166
Motocross, 150
Muzeo, 166, 174, 176, 177
Native American, 16, 28-31
Newport Beach, 34
Nieto, 34
No Doubt, 170
Nobel Prize, 168
Northrop Corp, 128
Nortronics Corp, 128
Ohio, 92
Ontiveros, 35, 36, 46
Opera House, 84, 167
Orange, 13, 14, 21, 23, 28, 31, 34, 67, 69, 71, 75, 76, 78, 79, 88, 90, 95, 96, 99, 100, 106, 107, 127, 129, 133, 135, 142, 145, 146, 156
Orso, 168
Ortega, 22, 24
Ortega Highway, 24
Ostrich, 79
Padres, 22, 27, 29, 30, 40
Palm, 94, 101, 130, 144, 146, 162, 165
Pasadena, 176
Patin, 121
Pearl Harbor, 124
Pearson, 104, 168

194

# About the Author

**Gail Eastman,** *Historian*

Born in Kalamazoo, Michigan, Gail grew up in Portage, Michigan. In 1979, she and her family moved to Orange County and, in 1982, settled in Anaheim. Gail attended Western Michigan University and, after moving to Orange County, earned her AA degree from Fullerton College.

Over the years she has worked in a variety of professions, from being a small business owner to holding executive management positions. She has a wide variety of interests, ranging from gardening and decorating, to researching and writing historic surveys of Anaheim's buildings for the City/State/National Historic Registery.

Gail has always been involved as a volunteer in church and civic activities, which lead her to be part of the group responsible for creating Anaheim's first recognized historic district in 1997. That began her education in Anaheim history.

She has served on the board of directors of the Anaheim Historic Society and has worked for the city of Anaheim, documenting, and photographing historic houses in support of historic preservation. Her work helped lay a foundation with the city for a full-time position to oversee historic preservation in Anaheim.

After leaving her job with the city in 2001, Gail was appointed to the Anaheim City Planning Commission and recently completed her third consecutive year as the Chairman.

Gail enjoys antiques, old houses, and old cars, especially traveling and discovering them in interesting places. All things historic rate high on her scale of fun activities.

She married the boy next door and they have three adult sons and four grandchildren.

# About the Contributors

## Bob Bates, *Artist*

Bob Bates is an artist of many talents. For years he has been known for his paintings of rustic Americana. Many of these paintings can be found in his first two Walter Foster books, *Adventure in Acrylics* and *More Adventures in Acrylics*.

Bob is a native Californian with a heritage that goes back to the early Carmel Mission era and the Gold Rush days. He and his wife, Valerie, live in Whittier, California where they are in the antique business. Currently, Bob spends much of his time creating illustrations of hotels, inns, restaurants and amusement parks across America.

## Helen Butler, *Graphic Designer*

Helen Butler was born in Inglewood, California. She has lived on both sides of the United States but mostly in La Habra and Fullerton. Helen attended Rosary High School in Fullerton. With an AA in Advertising Design from Fullerton College, this award winning designer started her own graphics company and works with clients locally and worldwide.

An active member of the community, she has volunteered her services with youth sports, local schools and community services.

Helen enjoys skydiving, snow skiing, traveling, and family activities with her husband and son, both named Rhett. Her passion is artwork and she still remembers her first drawings and art projects from pre school and kindergarten.

# Ordering Books

TESORO
PUBLISHING

## Order Online at
## www.tesoropublishing.com

Tesoro Publishing
P.O. Box 528, Fullerton, CA 92836-0528,